The Pastor's Competency Manual

Pastor Jerry E. Johnson Sr.

Southern California First Jurisdiction
Church of God in Christ
Pastors and Elders Council
Chairman - Administrative Assistant,
Superintendent Jerry Johnson
Dr. Garon Harden

Copy Right 2014

Submit Orders To:

Just Move On
135 Victoria Street
Long Beach, California 90805
Phone: 562-423-8653
Web-Site: www.justmoveon.org

OR
Lily Of The Valley Worship Center
888 E. Research Dr.
Suite 109
Palm Springs, California 92262
Phone: 760-323-4455
Web-Site: www.lilyofthevalleyworshipcenter.org

ISBN-13: 9781507768761
ISBN-10: 1507768761

Table of Contents

	Dr. Harden Foreword	v
	Bishop Charles E. Blake Sr. Presiding Bishop of the Church of God In Christ Forward	vii
	Introduction	ix
Chapter 1.	Leader-Member Exchange Theory (LMX)	1
Chapter 2.	Servant Leadership Theory	3
Chapter 3.	Motivation Theories	7
Chapter 3a.	Ethical Motivations in the Leader	9
Chapter 4.	Decision-Making Models	13
Chapter 5.	Conflict Resolution	17
Chapter 5a.	Biblical Principles: How Leaders Resolve Conflict	21
Chapter 6.	"Pareto Principle" The 80:20 Rule	27
Chapter 7.	The Making of a Good Leader	29
Chapter 8.	The Spiritual Lifestyle of a Leader	35
Chapter 9.	What Followers are Expecting from Leaders	39

Chapter 10.   People Skills How to Cultivate Good Relationships 43

Chapter 11.   Transformational Leadership 49

Chapter 12.   Organizational Culture and Leadership 53

Chapter 13.   Organizational Change Theory 57

Chapter 14.   Who is Qualified to Lead? 61

Chapter 15.   How to Spot a Leader 63

Chapter 16.   The Cost of Effective Leadership 67

Chapter 17.   Biblical Principles That Will Help Leaders Reach Their Potential 71

Chapter 18.   Biblical Examples of Men Who Became Great Leaders through Good Mentoring 75

Chapter 19.   Decision: The Key of Leadership 83

Chapter 20.   How Leaders Perceive Themselves 87

Chapter 21.   "Clergy Self Care – Finding a Balance for Effective Ministry" 91

Chapter 22.   "Balancing the Demands of Ministry and Family" By; Michael Henderson .. 101

Articles of Incorporation of ABC-Church, Inc. 104

Bylaws of ABC-Church, Inc. 109

501 (c) (3) Non-Profit Religious Organizations Tax and Legal Issues for Churches 137

Dr. Harden Foreword

I started preaching in October 1965, at my home church Westside Temple COGIC in Blytheville Arkansas when I was 18 years old. I had only been saved about a year and all I knew was that God called me to preach His Word and like most people who are called, I did not want to do it.

In those days, there were not any theological Seminaries I could attend, even if I could afford it. Our only resources for learning to preach God's Word were what we read from the Bible and occasionally what we read from another person's book.

After 49 years of preaching (I served 13 years as a Junior Pastor [that's what we were called then], and 34 years of pastoring), "My soul looks back and wonders how I go over!"

After so many up's and downs, fumbling and half-heartedly attempting to do things that I really didn't know how to do, I started attending seminars and finally in 1991 I was led to attend Southern California Community Bible College. I was able to complete and graduate from Bible College in June 19, 1994 after which I decided to continue Bible College where I received a Doctor of Divinity. In 1999, I returned to school to pursue a Ph.D. in Family Christian Counseling and a Master of divinity from "Ministerial Training Institute, in Inglewood, California. In 2008, Glendale University conferred upon me a Master of Science in Psychology and a Ph.D. in Theology. To this date, I am continuing to update my training in order to serve the kingdom of God and God's people.

Our purpose for this book serves to help guide men/women who are called to minister to this deeply distressed and troubled world.

We provide examples of how to rightly divide the Word of God in all situations. Whether you are a Pastor, Ordained Elder, Minister, Sunday School Teacher, Deacon/Deaconess or a Lay Member, this book will serve as a great tool for you. It is written for those who are just beginning to those who have been in ministry for years.

We're never too old to learn. Ask Moses, he was eighty years old when God called him. His assignment was to lead the Children of Israel out of Egypt. Moses did not have any materials to assist him, so God was his tutor as He is ours today. Through His Spirit and books that He inspires men/women to write, we have the help we need to guide us in the right direction when ministering to His people and fulfill our mission in the World and in the Body of Christ.

If you are facing challenges in the ministry that God has assigned you to, be it pastoral leadership, evangelizing, training others for leadership or just being a good servant for God, this is a tool that will assist you through those challenging times. We have highlighted several ensamples of men who have pioneered great ministries, most of whom are still living to tell of it. I believe these people shared their life experiences for my benefit and yours as well.

I am grateful for Administrative Assistant Jerry Johnson who contributed so much of his experience and labor in God's vineyard over the years to help develop ministers (both young and seasoned) to do the work of the Lord.

Now it is time for you to take your journey and explore the excitement awaiting you as you travel through this God inspired book.

Garon Harden, Ph.D

Bishop Charles E. Blake Sr.
Presiding Bishop of the Church of God In Christ
Forward

THE PASTOR'S COMPETENCY MANUAL FOR PRESENT & FUTURE PASTORS compiled by Dr. Garon Harden and Administrative Assistant Jerry E. Johnson Sr. is the first collaboration of these two experienced pastors and is long overdue. An intelligent compilation of knowledge and counsel for pastors/leaders, this book yields a comprehensive tool for those who presently serve as pastors and those who anticipate becoming pastors/leaders in the future.

In order to fulfill our purpose to lead effectively in ministry, we have to be in the will of God. As God has commissioned pastors to lead as a shepherd leads his sheep, it is essential that we primarily continue to avail ourselves to the counsel of the Holy Spirit and employ the resources provided for spiritual growth, and spiritual health.

Throughout Scripture, we see a continual call to seek those of skill and competency. The Lord told Moses in Exodus 31: 1-5 that He chose men "filled with the Spirit of God, with skill, ability and knowledge. Proverbs 22:29 says, "Do you see a man skilled in his work? He will stand before kings; He will not stand before obscure men." This book is designed to assist pastors/leaders in becoming more conversant with the qualities of a skillful and effective leader. Each section of this manual provides the reader with clear directives and tools on how to increase their leadership abilities by presenting such topics as

- Biblical Principles/How Leaders Resolve Conflict
- The Making of a Good Leader
- The Spiritual Lifestyle of a Leader
- Biblical Principles that Will Help Leaders Reach Their Full Potential
- Who is Qualified to Lead
- Clergy Self Care Finding a Balance for Effective Ministry

In serving as the Jurisdictional Prelate of First Ecclesiastical Jurisdiction of Southern California, Church of God in Christ from 1985 - 2009, I worked with both Administrative Assistant Jerry E. Johnson Sr., and Dr. Garon Harden, watching the Lord elevate them in their respective offices as pastors/leaders. Administrative Assistant Jerry E. Johnson Sr. currently serves as Chairman of Pastors' and Elders' Council for First Ecclesiastical Jurisdiction of Southern California and Administrative Assistant to Jurisdictional Prelate, Bishop Joe L. Ealy. Dr. Garon Harden serves as Regional Superintendent for the West Los Angeles Region under the First Jurisdiction. Both men are faithful servants of the Lord who are committed to the work of the ministry and continually exhibit a sincere passion for promoting education and leadership enrichment.

As we embark on challenges in our roles as leaders, let us recall our responsibilities as servants one to another, utilizing the principles of this book as they pertain to the Word of God, that we may do all things decent and in order.

I rejoice as we are presented with **THE PASTOR'S COMPETENCY MANUAL** FOR PRESENT **& FUTURE PASTORS."**

Pastors/Leaders, I encourage you to continue to focus on a promising future, while considering the affirmation of the Apostle Paul in Philippians 1:6, "Being confident of this very thing that he which hath begun a good work in you will perform it until the day of Jesus Christ."

In His Service

Charles E. Blake Sr.

Introduction

What precipitated me (Pastor Jerry E. Johnson Sr., a Pastor in the Church of God in Christ) to assemble this manual was being appointed Chairman of the Pastors and Elders Council of First Ecclesiastical Jurisdiction of Southern California. My interaction with many of the Pastors and Elders exposed the need for continued education.

To become an Elder in the Church of God in Christ, I had to attend a class and be tested before I was ordained. After ordination I received a certificate and the constitution book of COGIC. However, when I was appointed to the Pastorate I received a Pastor's certificate only.

Fortunately, I had a great foundation afforded me through my Pastor (Pastor Billie E. Johnson, also my Father). He spared no pain in teaching me about Ministry. I became his Youth Leader, Sunday School Superintendent, Choir Director, Member of the Trustee Board, District Youth Leader, State Public Relation Director, State Youth President etc. All of these positions prepared me for future leadership. I also had the opportunity to sit with him to probe his mind on the things he had learned during his many years of Ministry. I felt like Paul sitting at the feet of the Sanhedrin court.

On July 10, 1992 I was appointed Pastor of Lily of the Valley Church of God in Christ in Palm Springs California by Bishop Charles E. Blake Sr. During this time he was the Jurisdictional Prelate of First Ecclesiastical Jurisdiction of Southern California who now holds the office of Presiding Bishop of the Church of God in Christ. Under his tutelage, I was able to receive insight on becoming a leader of integrity. His main objective of leadership was ***"NEVER STOP LEARNING - READ!"***

I was the youngest Superintendent in the Jurisdiction, appointed to many committees and boards and had the privilege of working on the campaign committee to elect Bishop Charles Blake Sr. Presiding Bishop of the Church of God in Christ.

After Bishop Blake became the Presiding Bishop of the Church of God in Christ he relinquished his position as Jurisdiction Prelate. Superintendent Joe L. Ealy became the Jurisdictional Prelate. Under this administration I was elected the Chairman of the Pastors and Elders Council. In this position it became clear to me that all Pastors and Elders were not as fortunate as I to have two great leaders in my life which afforded me a solid foundation. In this position I have surmised our Pastors and Elders can't become 21st century leaders when they are vulnerable to law-suits which can be costly and can hinder their ability to devote the necessary time to building the Kingdom of God.

Therefore, *"THE PASTOR'S COMPENTECY MANUAL" was birthed in my spirit.* This manual is a guide for New Pastors and Elders aspiring to become Pastors and are ordained for pastoral ministry, to assist in the call to serve God and to carry out the ministry of Jesus Christ in the local church. In addition, this manual can assist Denominational officials in working with Local Pastors. **It is not intended to be the final authority** on a situation or condition, but it is to serve as a practical and understandable resource in the ministry of the Local Pastor. **This manual should never be cited as an authoritative source to support a particular position or viewpoint on an issue.**

Leadership is the compass of living. No subject has been more explored in our day than leadership.

Leadership comes in all varieties; good and bad, effective and ineffective, positive and negative or right or wrong. This manual will be looking at leadership from the standpoint of the Bible, in the Old and New Testaments, along with effective ancient and modern leadership principles.

Leader's success, fulfillment and happiness depend on our ability to relate effectively. The best way to become a leader that others are drawn to is to develop qualities that we are attracted to in others. What's the key to relating to others—it's putting yourself in someone else's place, instead of putting them in their place.

"EVERY CHRISTIAN WHO DESIRES TO BECOME A LEADER, MUST FIRST KNOW HOW TO FOLLOW"

The purpose of this manual is to present principles which will help Pastors, Denominational officials and Church Leaders through proven Biblical principles reach their full potential for God's purpose in their lives.

Thank you to the following committee members; Dr. Garon Harden, Pastor Bobby Davis, Pastor Michael Mancha, Pastor Phillip Washington, Pastor Gerald Johnson and Honorary Member Bishop Joe L. Ealy.

CHAPTER 1

Leader-Member Exchange Theory (LMX)

In-group/Out-group
Leader-member exchange (LMX) theory, developed by Dansereau, Graen, and Haga (1975) emphasized the dyadic (two person) relationships between leaders and followers. Those that were linked only by defined roles, job descriptions, and formal contracts were the out-group, and those that were linked by expanded and mutually-negotiated role responsibilities were the in-group. In each case, the leader and the follower formed an individualized working relationship (vertical dyad) that had its own unique characteristics.

Two Types of Relationships
In-group members have a common bond and value system that lends itself toward greater interaction with the leader. Research generally supports that leaders in these relationships give more challenging assignments and greater emotional support. These members are more dependable, have more communication with the leader, and have higher job performance and satisfaction than the out-group. Relationships in the positive dyads result in mutual trust, respect, and reciprocal influence. Conversely, out-group members have less in common with the leader and generally receive less information, influence, and fewer challenging assignments. Communication is formalized and production is confined to the job description.

Leadership Making
Graen and Uhl-Bien (1991) also discovered that positive relationships could create networks of mutual exchange and influence, which they called leadership making. This most recent approach recommends that leaders develop high quality relationships with all employees in the work unit, as well as a network of mutually-influencing throughout the organization. The LMX researchers recognized that there would be phases in the relationship as the leader and follower develop trust and respect for one another and eventually for the good of the group.

The ideas in LMX can be used throughout all levels of an organization since it draws attention to the importance of communication in leadership and helps leaders be aware of the uniqueness of each employee.

Implications for Church Leadership

The very notion of an in-group and an out-group is repugnant to most Christian thinking. However, we all know such groups generally exist in the church. They are not always developed by the pastor/leader, but usually exist before the pastor arrives. A new pastor at a church frequently studies the leadership landscape among the laity to discover who makes up the current influential in-group, then gets about either working with that group or gradually creating another in-group. Though the notion of in- and out-groups appears contrary to Christian values, we must admit that even Jesus had His group of seventy and even a smaller group of twelve apostles who formed the in-group among His followers. (In fact, some argue Jesus even had a smaller, more intimate in-group comprised of Peter, James and John.) Perhaps today's Christian resistance to the in- and out-group notion springs more from individual values other than biblical tradition. Nevertheless, LMX theory has significant implications for church leadership, some of which may include the following:

1. Church leadership is more than the leader's actions. It also includes the complex interactions between the leader and the followers.

2. LMX suggests good leaders are not automatically consistent in their leader relationships. In fact, a leader should operate differently with different people-in which case intentional inconsistency is good.

3. On arrival at a new church, an in-group probably already exists, possibly one established by the previous pastor. A new pastor will probably work with this in-group at first and then gradually develop a revised in-group. Those previously part of the in-group, who find themselves now a part of the out-group often cause trouble for the pastor.

4. Church leaders develop individuals. The very term "pastor" denotes shepherding. Individualized attention is not strange to a good shepherd. **<u>A church leader must see their task as developing the people more than growing a church</u>**. Spiritual formation—forming Christ in a community—is the pastor's work. To do that requires attention to both communal aspects of holiness and individual development of each member of the body. Church leaders should rise above "filling jobs" in their personnel program. *{A good transformational leader does not start with empty jobs and then seek people to fill them. He starts with each person's gifts, passions, abilities, personality and experiences and then attempts to develop that person through service in and out of the church}*.

CHAPTER 2

Servant Leadership Theory

Robert Greenleaf is often credited for initiating the current interest in servant leadership. Greenleaf (1977) saw business leaders as needing to serve society more constructively than merely by increasing profits for the company. He felt "business exists as much to provide meaningful work to the person as it exists to provide a product or service to the customer.

The philosophy of leading by serving has been explained by countless leadership theorists to include building an environment that not only serves the needs of the organization, but also provides a climate for its workers to grow and develop as human beings. After strict usage of the Delphi method, Laub (1999) developed a functional definition of servant leaders and servant-led organizations:

Servant Leaders and Servant-led Organizations

- Value People: by listening receptively, serving the needs of others first and trusting people.
- Develop People: by providing opportunities for learning, modeling appropriate behavior and building up others through encouragement.
- Build Community: by building strong relationships, working collaboratively and valuing individual differences.
- Display Authenticity: by integrity and trust, openness and accountability and a willingness to learn from others.
- Provide Leadership: by envisioning the future, taking initiative and clarifying goals.
- Share Leadership: by creating a shared vision, sharing decision-making power and sharing status and privilege at all levels of the organization.

Though servant leadership has many parallels with transformational leadership, it differs in leader focus. Transformational leaders build commitment in followers toward organizational objectives; ***servant leaders' highest value is the people, and organizational results are secondary outcomes.*** "Serving is not the means by which to get results, but the behavior of serving is the result". Servant leadership remains an intuitive-based theory because little empirical (observable; testable as experienced) evidence of servant-leader behavior exists. Nevertheless, the term servant leadership appears to be more than the sum of the words service and leadership. The concept continues to be influential in the future, especially in the leadership of learning organizations.

Implications for Church Leadership

Servant leadership theory can hardly be rejected by a Church built on the life, death and resurrection of Jesus Christ. Jesus Christ was the ultimate example of servant hood, by leaving all the glory of heaven to come as a human and accepting the way of the cross. His earthly ministry built up a Church that spread the gospel to the ends of the earth after He ascended into heaven again. The Church of the man who wrapped a towel about Himself to wash His own disciple's feet as His final lesson to them certainly cannot reject servant leadership as a proper approach to leading others. Not out loud at least. But in practice, servant leadership may be no more common in a church and in Christian organizations than it is in secular corporations. While church leaders salute Jesus Christ as the model servant-leader, and affirm the servant-leader approach loudly, in actual operation many church leaders practice leadership "as Gentiles" do (Matthew 20:25-28) in real life. Some of the implications of servant leadership theory for church leaders may be:

1. Church leaders must value people, for they are God's handiwork. Listening to people is important in the church. This is how the Holy Spirit guides the church-through its people, not just through the designated leader.

2. Church leaders must be people-developers more than program-pushers. The church-based servant-leader starts with the people, not the program. People development is the church's product.

3. The church does not make a product, it is the product. Churches don't just have pizza parties to attract new people-they do this to build community, to become what the church is to be: a community of the saints. Community building is a primary task of the church leader.

4. Church leaders must be authentic people who inspire trust. Talking about big dreams for the people to follow isn't enough; people follow leaders, not dreams. And they follow leaders with trustworthy integrity.

5. Leaders in the church must be men and women of vision, seeing the future and clarifying goals. In the church vision isn't just a picture of a bigger church or larger congregation.

It is a picture of God's kingdom as it should be and seeing one local church's part in that vision.

6. Church leaders should help their followers see God's vision directly from God, not just from the pastor. The followers can be trusted with decision-making power on how that church can become what God desires. After all, the clergy do not get filled with a different Holy Spirit than the laity.

NOTES

NOTES

CHAPTER 3

Motivation Theories

Several popular theories of motivation are discussed in the leadership literature and are usually based on a psychological explanation that helps leaders and managers better understand their workers.

LEARNED NEEDS THEORY-David McClelland's (1962) early work stated that many human needs are acquired from the culture, specifically the need for achievement, the need for affiliation, and the need for power. When a need is strong, individuals will choose behavior that meets that need. Such needs were developed from coping with their environment and tend to occur more often when behavior is rewarded more frequently. This theory also complements the views of situational leadership theory that may focus on task and/or relationship management.

THEORY X AND THEORY-Douglas McGregor (1960) believed that managers hold certain assumptions about people in organizational settings. Theory X meant that people are basically lazy, require structure and direction. Without it, they will act irresponsibly. Theory Y assumes that people is not lazy, do not have to be closely supervised and want to work, especially when it is meaningful and challenging. Argyris and Schon (1982), argue that leaders need to take care that they do not treat others with Theory Y statements (espoused theory) and then behave with Theory X assumptions (theory in action).

EXPECTANCY THEORY-Victor Vroom's (1964) theory of motivation is a more complex theory. His theory is based on the assumption that most behavior is under the voluntary control of the person. Behavior is related to outcome and success, however the value and attractiveness of these outcomes varies from one to another.

POSITIVE REINFORCEMENT-B.F. Skinner (1948) emphasized the external situation in his approach to personality and motivation. The Skinnerian view is an extreme behaviorist approach and sees an individual as a rather passive victim of events in his or her environment. Most theories of motivation support the belief that leaders can influence the motivation state of others. When leaders take an active role in motivating others, they are being sensitive to the motivational needs, as well as seeking to provide different structures for need satisfaction outside.

Implications for Church Leadership

Motivation is a concern for church leaders because part of their job is to motivate people to do the right thing. Churches are always seeking volunteers to work in the nursery, or youth sponsors, or are trying to get their members to fulfill the Great Commission (Matthew 28:19-20). Pastors and church leaders have to be motivators. And most realize that intrinsic motivation is more powerful and long lasting than extrinsic motivation. However, there is theological reason why ministers should care, not just about whether the people are motivated but why. In Christian thinking, the quality of a deed (or service) is not based on the deed itself but on the motivation. This notion is most prominent in the teaching of Jesus on the hypocrites praying publicly (Matthew 6:1-18). If their motivation was to be seen and praised, they received no reward in Heaven. Thus, Christian leaders must have considerable concern not only that people will be motivated to do a right deed or service, but that they will be motivated for the right reasons. Therefore, theories of motivation are highly relevant for church leaders.

Some implications of the above theories of motivation for church leadership may be:

1. Church leaders must be aware of what motivates people if they intend to get volunteers to respond. Churches have always been aware of motivating people, but a leader who is conscious of how to motivate them, can be more effective at getting people to respond. For example, people want to belong—to be a part of an exciting group (affiliation). People want to be a part of something worthwhile that is moving forward, making a contribution (achievement). And people want to participate in decision-making, be in on the action, have a vote, and be given authority (power). These three motivators are human motivators, thus they are factors in motivation of all church members. <u>Knowing and using them enables a church leader to more effectively multiply their leadership.</u>

2. It may be that individual churches specialize in promoting one basic motivation excessively while ignoring the power of the other intrinsic and extrinsic factors. If so, leaders in these churches might consider monitoring their motivational message to ensure balance.

3. It is also possible that an individual pastor or church leader might be inclined to motivate others using the motivator that he would be most motivated by. Such overuse of this motivational assumption may be an indicator of the most powerful motivator in the leader's life. Additionally, recognizing which is the master motivator for an individual leader, and an examination of what may not motivate him, may help the leader develop a broader approach to the motivation of others. "Know thyself" is good advice at this point.

CHAPTER 3A

Ethical Motivations in the Leader

Most leadership literature assumes a need for some form of power in the leader. Harvard social psychologist, David McClelland (1987) found that effective leadership is motivated by a set of three learned motivations: affiliation, power and achievement. Kanungo and Mendonca (1996) applied these three motivations to build an ethical model for leaders. They suggested both a positive and negative expression for each of McClelland's motivations. McClelland's three motivations and the Kanungo and Mendonca positive/negative expressions are shown in the following list:

- *Affiliation*: need for friendship and social contact.
    - Negative: Avoidance; clings for fear of rejection
    - Positive: Approaching; as in concern for others
- *Achievement:* need for production, responsibility, realizing goals, solving problems.
    - Negative: Personal gain only
    - Positive: Social achievements or collective capability
- *Power:* need for impact, authority, pressure, winning arguments.
    - Negative: Personal; emphasizing dominance and submission, and self-aggrandizement
    - Positive: Institutional; persuasive and inspirational for purposes of the organization

Kanungo and Mendonca suggest that altruism is the value that drives the positive—versus the negative—expression in each of the above categories. Altruism (intent is to benefit others) is thus the antidote to a negative egotistic motivation (intent is to benefit self), as it moderates or overcomes the effects of the negative option for each intrinsic motivation. The authors observed *"organizational leaders are consistently effective only when they are motivated by concern for others even when it results in some cost to self".* In order for a leader to achieve such an altruistic vision for their organization and the people in it, the authors stress the following process:

1; *Assessing the Environment*. Instead of focusing their own inward needs and not considering followers' needs, turn outward and focus on the welfare of the whole organization.

2; ***Casting the Vision.*** After formulating a vision for the good of the organization, be willing to assume the risk of seeing the potential in all followers and articulating the vision in a way they can understand.

3; ***Implementing the Plan.*** Through encouragement (the courage), empowering (shared decision-making), and modeling (taking the risk of sacrifice), people can be effective leaders. Motivations are not fixed on attributes, according to McClelland (1977), but can be learned, unlearned, and changed. He believes that the formation of a positive motivation happens only as the leader matures through developmental stages.

Leadership is more than a position. It is a moral relationship between people, held together by loyalty and trust, and rooted in the leader's commitment to values and accountability when exercising power and authority. This requires leaders to be ethical and consistent in their espoused values (words) as well as their behavior (deeds).

Implications for Church Leadership

For church leaders, the motivation should be and is as important as the result. William Law and John Wesley (and Jesus long before) believe right intentions are even more important than right actions. The Pharisees of Jesus' day were condemned by Jesus not for their wrong actions of praying or fasting, but for their wrong motivations (to be seen and praised by others-Matthew 6). The church leader can say, "Well, it worked and we grew, so it is good" in defending that the ends justify the means. A leader might say this, but to God the motivation is as important as the result, or more so. Research on ethical motivations helps church leaders face and ponder their own motivation for leading the church. Perhaps we can't simply say this leader has a good motivation while that one has a bad motivation. More likely we all have mixed motives and periodically doing self-examination and sorting of our motives is good Christian self-leadership. Some of the implications of ethical motivations research for church leaders may be:

1. Why do you want to succeed? The research in U.S. businesses shows three primary motivations: to be part of a great group of people (affiliation); to accomplish something great (achievement) or to make a real impact in life (power). These three classic motivations may be a factor in what attracts ministers to leadership in the church. Which is the more powerful motivating factor for you? Which is the greatest motivator for you?

2. Each of the three motivations has both a positive and a negative manifestation. Church leaders should put aside relationship-avoidance or excessive clinging relationships (negative affiliation). They should resist temptation to work only for personal gain and career development (negative achievement). And they should reject the impulse to build a personal kingdom of power (negative power). Rather, a Christian church

leader should steer their motivations toward the positive side of these three: building strong other-oriented social groups (positive affiliation), working for the collective achievements of the local church (positive achievement) and building the institution of the church and kingdom of God (positive power).

*warp change gets the credit for the shift, but is often unable to tell what secret measures brought on the "tipping point". (In the church, however, the extraordinary blessing and action of the Holy Spirit must always be factored in, for the Spirit can always bring the church to the "tipping point".

NOTES

NOTES

CHAPTER 4

Decision-Making Models

Vroom and Yetton proposed a series of procedures for making decisions, ranging from a unilateral directive decision by the leader without input, to highly participatory forms of decision-making. Theirs was an early decision flow process model designed to help a leader determine whether directive or participative decision-making would be more appropriate. This deductive approach to decision-making assumes that no one style is best for all situations. The choice depends on whether the leader is aiming for decision quality or subordinates' acceptance of the decision, or some combination of these. The Vroom and Yetton model had six decision procedures, summarized as follows:

Autocratic decision-making
1. ***Decide.*** The leader solves the problem with the information at hand.
2. ***Collect information and decide.*** The leader collects information from subordinates and then makes the decision.

Consultation decision-making
3. ***Share problem individually, collect ideas, and decide.*** The leader shares the problem individually with followers, gathers suggestions and then makes the decision.
4. ***Share the problem with the group, collect ideas, and decide.*** The leader shares the problem with subordinates as a group, reflecting their collective ideas and then makes the decision.

Group participative decision-making
5. ***Share problem individually, collect alternative solutions and consensus decision.*** The leader shares the problem individually, generating alternative solutions, and attempts to reach consensus on a decision.
6. ***Share problem with group, develop alternative solutions and consensus decision.*** The leader shares the problem guiding the group to generate alternative solutions, attempting to reach consensus as a group on a decision.

A year later, Vroom and Jago (1974) added a seventh choice to the above list, Delegated decision-making:

<u>Delegated</u> decision-making

7. ***Delegate the problem, support subordinate's solution.*** The leader delegates the entire problem to a subordinate and gives responsibility and support for his or her solution Vroom and Yetton provided seven questions to help diagnose the demands of the situation. The Yes or No answers determine what decision style to use by eliminating one or more of the options from the directive/participative continuum above. (This process was later diagramed as a <u>decision tree</u> by Vroom). The questions, referred to as "**<u>7 Rules</u>**," are:

1. Does the problem possess a quality requirement?
2. Does the leader have sufficient information to make a high-quality decision?
3. Is the problem structured?
4. Is acceptance of the decision by subordinates important for effective implementation?
5. If the leader were to make the decision alone, are they reasonably certain that it would be accepted by subordinates?
6. Do subordinates share the organizational goals to be attained in solving this problem?
7. Is conflict among subordinates likely in preferred solution?

Implications for Church Leadership

Decision-making in the church is not merely a matter of who has the power and what might be the best thing to do. Instead, deciding has theological implications. If a church is deciding whether to stay downtown in their present facility and minister to their current neighborhood, or move out to the suburbs to minister to new housing developments, it is trying to decide theologically, What is God's will? Churches assume there is such a thing as God's will in their decisions, at least the important ones. Seeking God's will is thus part of the process in Christian decision-making.

The point is that the decision-making power is a theological matter to the church and thus a church leader must maintain their theology integrity as they manage the decision-making process. Some of the implications of Vroom and Yetton's decision-making models for church leaders may be:

1. Few pastors can run their church as if they were the owner-manager. Therefore, a pastor usually must become a master at **"<u>managing the decision-making process,</u>" not the master <u>decision-maker.</u>**

2. Pastors should avoid manipulation of the decision-making process. Local church decision-making power (for key decisions, at least) is often given to the members, yet the pastor is the trained professional leader and often knows which is the best solution. Therefore, a challenging situation often develops in church leadership. The pastor knows the best solution, but does not have the power to decide. In these situations,

the pastor may set up a process that looks very much like the participatory decision-making process, but in reality is a process where the pastor can manipulate the local board into deciding what the pastor has already pre-determined is the right decision. If all goes smoothly, nobody will notice. But if the hidden solution of the pastor receives resistance, the pastor's manipulation of the process often becomes more evident and the laity feels manipulated. How does a pastor avoid this predicament? Usually a pastor can bring laity into the decision-making process—at the consultative level even before the pastor has determined what the decision should be. While manipulative leadership can make things happen for a time, eventually it will erode the pastor's credibility as a leader and ultimately it is counterproductive.

3. In large churches, the pastor may use this process more with staff than the board. The decision-making process in larger mega-churches is different than that of average-size churches. *(No matter what the polity, decision-making power in large churches often gravitates to the full-time paid staff.)*

   <u>**What was once done by the board or committees is now done by the professional staff.**</u> In these churches, sometimes the board becomes more like a College Board of Trustees, dealing mostly with financial issues and replacing the senior pastor when they resign or need to leave for other reasons. Thus, in larger churches the decision-making process outlined above often reflects the senior pastor's role with staff ministers and therefore it has more in common with the business process from which these models emerged. A senior pastor, for example, should determine which of the seven procedures will work best for decisions to be made about staff specialties, such as youth camp, the Easter pageant, or new Sunday school classes.

NOTES

NOTES

CHAPTER 5

Conflict Resolution

Conflict occurs in all segments of organizations. The question is not the existence of it, but rather character and intensity, plus the manner in which it is expressed, channeled, or camouflaged. Some authors prefer to call this managing conflict. Others, however, see the need for leadership in modeling how to handle conflict—and its related issues of power, values, and change—constructively, so that leader-follower needs and organizational goals are not jeopardized. In addition, <u>**many leaders see conflict as an opportunity to develop their followers.**</u>

Morton Deutsch's (1973) extensive research in the field has found that conflict between parties with cooperative rather than competitive relations is likely to be less destructive. Destructive conflict has a tendency to escalate and expand beyond the initial cause. Therefore, it is important for leaders to continually strengthen an environment of conflict-limiting factors, such as encouragement of creative thinking, commitment to cooperation, and "benevolent misperception" (minimizing differences vs. enhancing flaws)—all of which keep the conflict within bounds. Leaders must avoid negative competitive strategies and power tactics (e.g., threats, coercion, and deception), lack of communication, and oversensitivity. These can drive out the conflict-limiting factors listed earlier—if those are weak. Though it is an oversimplification of Deutsch's work, the truth of "cooperation breeds cooperation, while competition breeds competition" has many applications for leaders of organizations.

Gerald Goldhaber (1979), who wrote the seminal work on organizational communication, believes <u>**conflict is not inevitable, but a certain amount is highly desirable.**</u> Goldhaber primarily addresses group conflict, which can be within a group and tear apart or decrease its activity; or it may occur between groups, which may actually tend to bring members together and increase their activity. His recommendations generally include a time for each side to describe their own image and the perception of the other's view, then reporting this to their other group. After separate discussions of what may cause the discrepancy in the varying perceptions on the issue, the groups come together to suggest their alternative solutions/compromises for the problem. Furthermore, leaders will encourage planning on how to relate differently toward each other in the future.

Ken Sande (1997) addressed personal conflict resolution from his experience as a lawyer and as a Christian. He believed that lawsuits tend to drive people further apart, and there should be a better way. Peacemaker Ministries began in 1982 for resolving conflicts out of court in a cooperative rather than an adversarial (the legal system's) manner. In order to help people change the attitudes and habits that led to the conflict, he leads the involved parties through four basic stages:

1) Glorify God (1 Cor. 10:31) – showing a complete love for God and protecting from impulsive, self-centered behaviors that escalate conflict.
2) Get the log out of your eye (Matt. 7:5) – facing up to our own attitudes, faults, and responsibilities before pointing out what others did wrong.
3) Go and show your brother his fault (Matt. 18:15) – confronting constructively when others fail to accept responsibility for their actions; may require other neutral individuals to help restore peace.
4) Go and be reconciled (Matt. 5:24) – committing to restoring damaged relationships; requires forgiveness and cooperative negotiation.

Sande believes God's peacemaking principles may be applied in the home, workplace, church, and neighborhood. He expands on each with helpful questions for the leader to guide the parties through the process of conflict resolution.

Implications for Church Leaders

Jesus was the great peacemaker. In one of the Beatitudes, He blesses peacemakers, yet elsewhere Jesus also said He did not come to bring peace but a sword. Both Jesus and Paul offer specific instructions on handling conflict between believers in the church. The church, while reflecting a perfect body in Heaven, is essentially an earthly institution (where Martin Luther placed it in his scheme of things). As an earthly institution including less-than-perfect human beings with varied experiences, opinions and representing varied cultures, we can expect conflict in the church and among denominations. However, conflict in the church does not always issue from our human tendencies, but can also be prompted by supernatural influences. Division, strife, and sectarianism (e.g. being of Paul vs. Apollos) are sometimes condemned in Scripture as more than human frailties, but as sin and prompted by the Devil. Either way, church leaders will face conflict.

Experienced church leaders don't debate the existence of conflict so much as they try to determine how to avoid, resolve, or manage it. Some of the implications of conflict resolution theory for church leaders may be:

1. Every church leader must decide their view on conflict. Is conflict in the church something bad that should be avoided? Is conflict bad, but should be expected and resolved?

Or is conflict actually a good sign of health and diversity and should be managed by the church leader? Many church leaders have not determined their theological stance on conflict in the church. Most church leaders need more thought on their ecclesiology to determine where conflict fits in their view of the church. Once this decision is made, the church leader can approach conflict as resolving or managing it.

2. Goldhaber raises the question for church leaders as to the potential good results of conflict. Is there more conflict in a church that is changing, growing and doing new things than a church that is static, declining or predictable? To what extent is conflict between denominations or local churches actually a good thing? How can a church leader manage conflict in a way to produce greater gains for the Kingdom?

3. Ken Sande and Peacemaker Ministries provide a summary of the biblical approach to conflict management and resolution. This appears to be a formula presented by Jesus 2000 years ago that all churches and individuals can use today. What would a church look like that implemented these practices? How would a church implement these four steps and maintain them as practices in a local body? What about a senior pastor as the church leader who insists that people go to the "offending party" (soloist, Sunday school teacher, youth pastor) and complain directly. Does this approach ever border on shrinking responsibility as the church's leader? Does it squelch feedback?

4. Certainly, most effective church leaders learn the skills of practicing conflict-limiting practices, including high levels of cooperation instead of competition and power tactics, heavy emphasis on communication, creative thinking, and developing a culture of what Deutsch calls "benevolent misperception" (grace) to keep conflict from becoming destructive.

NOTES

NOTES

CHAPTER 5A

Biblical Principles: How Leaders Resolve Conflict

1. *<u>Difficulties for leaders usually come in two forms</u>;*
   1; Problems with the group, and 2) problems in their own personal lives. Storms are as much a part of life as starlight. A leader is not exempt from personal problems in life. Notice **2 Corinthians 2:4-6;** *"For if I make you sorry, who is he then that maketh you glad, but is the same which is made sorry by me?"* (Apostle Paul). *"Man that is born of a woman is of a few days, and full of trouble"* (Job).

According to Dr. John Maxwell, "confrontation is difficult"; two things have to happen for us to become better leaders, and both of them deal with confrontation:

   a. <u>We have to settle for the person or the group.</u>
   b. <u>We must do it in the spirit of love and both things have to happen.</u>
   - If a leader doesn't confront; they will never settle the major issues and they will never be the leader God wants them to be; and will also be operating on less than their potential.
   - If we don't confront in love, those that work for us, will not appreciate us, nor will they want to continue to work for us under those circumstances.

*Before a leader confronts anyone about a problem or situation, make sure it is not a problem you have in your own personal life. A question you should ask yourself: Is this an issue I need to deal with myself? It doesn't do any good spiritually to confront someone else about a problem we have in our own lives.

2. *<u>Biblical Principles: How leaders resolve conflicts</u>*
   Do you know it could be your own personal problem that influences you to confront the other person, anyway?

Luke 6:41; *"And why beholdest thou the mote that is in thy brother's eye, but perceives not the beam that is in thine own eye?"*
42; *"Either how canst thou say to thy brother, Brother, let me pull out the mote that is in thine eye, when thou thyself beholdest not the beam that is in thine own eye? Thou hypocrite, cast out first the beam out of thine own eye, and then shalt thou see clearly to pull out the mote that is in thy brother's eye."*

3. <u>Conflicts are unavoidable</u>

Conflicts are unavoidable because motion causes friction. If you lead people, then you must realize that you are going to deal with conflict. As pastors and church organizational leaders, our jobs consist of dealing with people. Confrontation will be something we will never completely eliminate from leading people and/or organizations.

You must realize when you are dealing with people—motion comes from friction; and the more people you have, the more friction you have to deal with. If you can settle issues and problems in your own life, confrontation will become easier for you, because you will come to realize that this is a part of your job.

According to Dr. John Maxwell, "In Joy Life Ministry," there are six reasons why it is difficult to confront:

1. Fear of being disliked – Nobody wants to be disliked; we want everybody to love us. Every time you have to confront someone, you risk someone disliking you.

2. The fear of rejection – We may be afraid that people will reject what we say. They may even leave the organization and spread the wrong information about us, withhold their tithes, offering, etc.

3. The fear of creating anger or a fear of making things worse – I do not believe that confrontation makes matters worse, however, I do believe what can make a situation worse is the spirit of confrontation. If you have a bad attitude and do not control your emotions, it can only make matters worse.

4. Phariseeism - Sometimes it is difficult to confront people about certain problems and issues, because we know that these very issues that we need to confront others on are problems in our own lives that we have not dealt with. You say to yourself, "How can I confront that person about this situation, when I know I have the same problem in my life?"

5. Sharing our feelings – A lot of confrontation is intuitive and expresses how we feel.

6. Lack of confrontation skills – Sometimes, the reason we don't confront others is because we haven't been taught confrontation skills. The leaders should never take the "winner take all" attitude. Leaders must be open-minded and never say there will be no compromise; that should never be your attitude in any confrontation. I have learned at several seminars, various ways handle conflicts.

    a. Many people walk away from conflicts.
    They want to keep the peace at all cost. I am not saying that there are right and wrong choices. Before I get in a difficult personal situation, first, I ask myself, "Am I holding back for my personal comfort, or for the good of the organization? Am I doing what makes me comfortable?" *"If I do what is good for the organization, and it happens to make me feel comfortable, I must remember that two wrongs do not make a right."* (Fred Smith) There are times we should walk away from conflict, but there are times we must confront.
    b. Sometimes we must stick our heads in the sand, and say, "It will go away."
    Surprisingly, many times this is the best option to consider. Leaders many times elevate insignificant incidents to the status of significant problems, simply by agreeing to discuss the matter further. The insightful leader needs to be aware of which incident should be handled this way and when one should not. Since most leaders are not looking for additional work, this option to confront can be useful.
    c. Wade around it
    Never deal with any issue or problem this way, because it is a bad way to resolve any conflict; an unresolved problem is still a problem.
    d. Many leaders wave the white flag or they just give up
    Quitting is a permanent solution to a temporary problem.
    e. Some leaders just "fight it out"
    There are some people that have the ability to make a mess out of every issue.
    f. The right way is to work it out!
    You need to work at the things that are important. A leader must be true to the scriptures, "Do unto others as you would have them do unto you."

As Christians, we should be concerned in a positive sense about others. Notice the following scriptures:

Philippians 2:4; *"Look not every man on his own things, but every man also on the things of others."*

Matthew 5:23; *"Therefore if thou bring thy gift to the altar, and there remembers that thy brother hath ought against thee."*

24; *"Leave there thy gift before the altar, and go thy way; first be reconciled to thy brother, and then come and offer thy gift."*

Hebrews 10:24; *"And let us consider one another to provoke unto love and to good works."*

Galatians 6:1; *"Brethren, if a man be over-taken in a fault, ye which are spiritual, restore such a one on the spirit of meekness; considering thyself, lest thou also be tempted."*

Ephesians 4:14; *"That we henceforth be no more children, tossed to and fro, and carried about with every wind of doctrine, by the sleight of men, and cunning craftiness, whereby they lie in wait to deceive;"*

15; *"But speaking the truth in love may grow up into him in all things, which is the head, even Christ:"*

When we have to confront, keep these things in mind:

1. <u>**Get a better understanding.**</u> To get a better understanding, you must know what's on the individual's mind. "In my preparation to reason with a man, we spend one-third of my time thinking about myself, and what I should say; and two-thirds thinking about him, and what he is going to say," quoted-Abraham Lincoln.

2. <u>**A positive change.**</u>
    a. It could be me

3. <u>**A growing relationship.**</u>
    a. As Christians, we confront not to embarrass, belittle, tear down or humiliate. We confront because of our commitment to help others reach their potential; including a full-fledged stature in Christ. Notice what Paul says;
    Colossians 1:10; *"That ye might walk worthy of the Lord unto all pleasing, being fruitful in every good work, and increasing in the knowledge of God;"*

4. <u>**We must always confront with the right spirit.**</u>
    Romans 1:10; *"Making request, if any means now at length I might have a prosperous journey by the will of God to come unto you."*

We must never confront because it makes us feel better. Being a leader, we are committed to the Lord and His goals for us. Therefore, it is part of our job to help our brother/sister to mature in Christ, with the right spirit.

Galatians 6:1; *"Brethren, if a man be overtaken in a fault, ye which are spiritual, restore such a one in the spirit of meekness; considering thyself, lest thou be tempted."*

2 Corinthians 10:1; *"Now I Paul myself beseech you by the meekness and gentleness of Christ, who in presence am base among you, but being absent am bold toward you."*

Always start on a positive note. Watch out when people say they agree with you in principle, it usually means they are getting ready to argue.

Learn to structure what you need in this order: WHAT describes what the other person is doing to cause you a problem? Example: "You're always talking about me." HOW, tells how this makes you feel. WHY, tells why this is important to you. Example: It causes me to cry or to become angry, etc.

5. *Always allow the person who is being confronted an opportunity to respond.*
   They will not be ready to listen to reason, until they have expressed their emotions or had time to swallow the hurt.

6. *Repeat or Rephrase the person's explanation.*
   This will help the confronted person to understand you know their position. Allow them to explain why they feel the confrontation was right or wrong.

7. *Indicate the desired action to be taken.*
   This places the focus on the future. The person who wants to change will gravitate toward the possibility of making things better.

8. *Reiterate the positive strength of the person.*
   What gets rewarded, gets done - #1 Management priorities.

9. *Put the issues in the past.*
   Never bring it up again, unless the problem reoccurs or you use it to affirm positive change and growth.

HOW TO SALVAGE A CONFRONTATION AMBUSH

1. *Nothing takes God by surprise.* God is omniscient – He knows everything; and if He allows it, there is a reason, and I can choose to benefit from it.
   a. Ask God for wisdom and ask for others' opinions.

James 1:5; *"If any of you lack wisdom, let him ask of God, that giveth to all men liberally, and Upbraided not; and is shall be given him."*

Separate the message from the messenger. It is difficult – the message is more important because of who said it, not what was said. **<u>Do not become emotionally involved.</u>** Don't be defensive.

Proverbs 1:15; *"My son, walk not thou in the way with them: refrain thy foot from their path;"*
Proverbs 12:1; *"Whoso loveth instruction loveth knowledge: but he that hateth reproof is brutish."*
Proverbs 12:15; *"The way of a fool is right in his own eyes: but he that hearkened unto counsel is wise."*
Proverbs 12:25; *"Heaviness in the heart of man maketh it stop: but a good word maketh it glad."*
Proverbs 23:12; *"Apply thine heart unto instruction, and thine ears to the words of knowledge."*
Proverbs 12:12; *"The wicked desireth the net of evil men: but the root of the righteous yielded fruit."*
Proverbs 28: 13; *"He that covereth his sins shall not prosper: but whoso confesseth and forsaketh them shall have mercy."*

2. **<u>Work in areas of truth.</u>** J. Oswald Sanders in his book, "Spiritual Leadership" says, *"Every call for help is by no means necessarily a call from God. For every such call cannot be responded to. If the Christian leader sincerely plans his day in the Lord's presence, and carries out that plan to the best of his ability (that's all that God requires), he then must leave it there. His responsibilities extend only to the matter or plan that lies within his control; the rest he can truthfully commit to his loving and competent heavenly father."*

3. **<u>All leaders should seek reconciliation</u>** {Romans 12:18}. Remember the goal for confrontation is a growing relationship. All leaders should become accountable to another (other) leader(s).

Ecclesiastes 4:9; *"Two are better than one; because they have a good reward for their labor."*

10; *"For if they fall, the one will lift up his fellow: but woe to him that is alone when he falleth; for he hath not another to help him up."*

12; *"And if one prevail against him, two shall withstand him; and a threefold cord is not quickly broken."*

Larry Crabb, in his book "Inside Out" says, *"Between the time when God gave us life, and the time when he provided all the joys this life brings, he intended to change us into people who can more deeply enjoy him now, and represent him well to others. The urgency required to make that change is always painful, but God will settle for nothing less than deep changes in our character and transformation, and restructuring of how we approach life."*

If leaders are willing to learn and implement these principles of biblical confrontation, it will lighten their load when they have to confront an individual or a group, in their organization.

CHAPTER 6

"Pareto Principle" The 80:20 Rule

Vilfredo Pareto (1848-1923) was an Italian economist who studied the distribution of wealth in a variety of countries in the early 1900s. He discovered a common phenomenon: about 80 percent of the wealth in most countries was controlled by a consistent minority, or about 20 percent of the people. Pareto called this a "predictable imbalance" i.e., <u>the relationship between input and output is rarely, if ever, balanced.</u>

In his 1950 book, The Quality Control Handbook, J.M. Juran first recognized the applicability of the Pareto principle to many fields. His particular focus was the quality defects in manufacturing and confirmed that relatively few defects accounted for their manufacturing problems. In honor of Pareto's original findings, he named this consistent mathematical relationship the Pareto Principle, now more commonly referred to as the 80:20 rule.

Richard Koch (1998) presented an analysis of Pareto's Principle as it applies to leadership and management. Koch argues this 80:20 rule is found in almost every part of modern life from stock investment to time management. He suggests that leaders and managers should find the highly leveraged 20% elements in an organization and pour their energy into these highly-productive people and activities that have influence beyond their apparent size. Thus, the 80:20 rule has been expanded far beyond its first economic use. ***<u>Leaders soon learn that a minority of people produce the majority of results.</u>***

Implications for Church Leaders

While one might quibble about the 80 percent or 20 percent (it is sometimes 60:40 or 90:10), the insight is broadly applied to leadership and management. The "80:20 rule" has become one of the best known leadership shorthand terms reflecting the notion that most of the results (of a life, of a program, of a financial campaign) come from a minority of effort (by people, or inputs). Some applications of the 80:20 rule in church leadership are:

80% of the work is usually done by 20% of the people.
80% of the problems are usually caused by 20% of the people.
80% of the value of my day is produced by 20% of the activity.
80% of my mentoring multiplication will likely come from 20% of the mentees.
80% of our new converts will probably come from 20% of the programs.
80% of the giving in a capital campaign often comes from 20% of the donors.
80% of the quality can be achieved in 20% of the time – perfection takes 5 times longer.

It is quite likely that Jesus worked with the assumption of the 80:20 rule, when He purposefully left the crowds to focus most of His time with the twelve apostles. He even has an inner circle of Peter, James and John whom He mentored more intensely. Admittedly, there are dangers of implementing 80:20 thinking all of the time, for example, life-threatening situations some families face or the evangelism opportunities that surface unexpectedly. However, when pastors set priorities for the year, they would do well to search for the 20 percent elements, i.e., those areas, efforts, programs, and people that are producing the most results in their overall ministry. Then church leaders can pour most of their energy into them.

NOTES

CHAPTER 7

The Making of a Good Leader

In 1990, Pastor Rick Warner did a seminar on "What it takes to be a Good Leader." He focused on eight biblical characteristics that would help develop good leadership skills when applied with the right spirit at the right time. These leadership principles are found in the book of Nehemiah.

The foundation of leadership is character-not charisma. Character consists of the disposition, nature, personality, and the distinctive quality of a person or thing. Charisma consists of the feature, technicality, difference, or any part of the facial expression that portrays as the main attraction.

The followings are eight characteristics given in the book of Nehemiah, and if they are administered in the proper manner and at the proper time, you will have a portion of what it takes to be a good leader.

1. *__Compassion:__ sympathy and tenderness*

Nehemiah 1:4; *"And it came to pass, when I heard these words, that I set down and wept and mourned certain days, and fasted, and prayed before the God of heaven."*

Nehemiah wept and mourned over Jerusalem, when he heard that the walls and the graves of his ancestors were destroyed. Compassion also has the connotation of a person's feelings, or putting themselves in someone's place, so that they may be able to feel what he or she feels at the time of their suffering. Nehemiah has compassion for his people when he heard the bad news.

Nehemiah 5:2-7
2; "For there were that said, we, our sons, and our daughters, are many: therefore we take up corn for them, that we may eat and live."

3; "Some also there were that said, we have mortgaged our lands, vineyards, and houses that we might buy corn for them, because of the dearth."

4; "There were also that said, we have borrowed money for the kin's tribute, and that upon our lands and vineyards."

5; "Yet now our flesh is as the flesh of our brethren, our children as their children, and lo, we bring into bondage our sons and our daughters to be servants, and some of our daughters are brought into bondage already, neither is it in our power to redeem them, for other men have our lands and vineyards."

6; "And I was very angry when I heard their cry and these words."

7; "Then I consulted with myself, and I rebuked the nobles, and the rulers, and said unto them, ye exact usury, every one of his brother, and I set a great assembly against them."

He reacted to the injustice that was administered to the poor. In verse 6 it states, "He was angry, he rebuked the nobles and the rulers for their mistreatment of the poor." He had compassion for the people, which is one of the characteristics of a good leader.

2. **_Contemplation:_** *To consider, meditate, reflect, view, purpose, and to propose. Nehemiah spent much time in prayer and meditation reflecting and thinking things through.*

Nehemiah 2:11-13
11; "So I came to Jerusalem, and was there three days."

12; "And I arose in the night, I and some few men with me, neither told I, any man what my God had put in my heart to do at Jerusalem. Neither was there any beast with me, save the beast that I rode upon."

13; "And I went out by night by the gate of the valley, even before the dragon – well, and to the dung port, and viewed the walls of Jerusalem, which were broken down, and the gates thereof were consumed with fire."

Nehemiah took a midnight ride around the city; he always took the time to think before speaking. In referring back to Nehemiah 5:7, *"Then I consulted with myself, and I rebuked the nobles, and the rulers and said unto them, yet exact usury, every one of his brother, and I set a great assembly against them."* Nehemiah made his plans to think it through, and he thought it through. (Other scripture references: Nehemiah 1:4-11; 2:4; 4:4-5,9;5:19; 6:9, and 13:14,22)

3. **_Consideration:_** *A point of importance, a thing worth considering, thinks about the advantages and disadvantages, to assess before reaching a decision.*

Nehemiah maintained a positive attitude. He had never been sad before the king.

Nehemiah 2:1; *"And it came to pass in the month Nisan, in twentieth year of Artaxerxes that wine was before him: and I took up the wine, and gave it unto the king. Now I had not been before time sad in his presence."*

God was the source of Nehemiah's strength.
Nehemiah 1:4; *"And it came to pass, when I heard these words, that I sat down and wept, and mourned certain days, and fasted, and prayed before the God of heaven."*

Read the whole chapter. Every good leader must be able to think out the advantages and disadvantages of any project before pursuing it.

4. <u>**Concentration**</u>: *Fix, aim, focus, and center-in.*

Notice Nehemiah 2:5-18
I.   Nehemiah always focused on his goals.
II. He devised a plan.
III. He organized the work (see Neh, 3:1-32).
IV. He refused to be distracted.

Nehemiah 6:3; *"And I sent messengers unto them, saying I am doing a great work, so that I cannot come down; why should the work cease, whilst I leave it, and come down to you?"*
4; "Yet they sent unto me four times after this sort; and I answered them after the same manner."

5. <u>**Creativity**</u>: *Effect, produce, design, visualize, and envision.*

Nehemiah was a problem solver as illustrated in Chapter 2:7, 8
7; "Moreover, I said unto the king, if it please the king, let letters be given me to the governors beyond the river, that they may convey me over till I come to Judah."

8; "And a letter unto Asaph the keeper of the king's forest, that he may give me timber to make beams for the gates of the palace which appertained to the house, and for the wall of the city, and for the house that I shall enter into, and the king granted me, according to the good hand of my God upon me."

Clearly, Nehemiah anticipated problems, yet remained focused. Every godly leader must learn how to stay focused on the project that God has assigned to him. When Sanballat heard that Nehemiah had the children of Israel rebuilding the wall, he became angry and mocked the Israelites saying, "What do these feeble Jews think? Do they think they can revive the stones out of the rubbish which are burned?" Then Tobiah the Ammonite was by him and he said, "Even that which they build if a fox go up he shall even break down their stone wall," Neh. 4:1-3. They continue to make threats against Nehemiah, but Nehemiah stayed focused on the project. He never left the work to meet with them. He assigned each father and son to set watch over their individual families. He posted them by families.

Notice **Nehemiah 4:13**, *"Therefore set I in the lower places behind the wall, and on the higher places, I even set the people after their families with their swords, their spears, and their bows."*
He created work shifts.

Nehemiah 4:16; *"And it came to pass from that time forth, that the half of my servants wrought in the work, and the other half of them held both the spears, the shields, and the bows, and the habergeons; and the rulers were behind all the house of Judah."*

17; *"They which builded on the wall, and they that bare burdens, with those that laded, everyone with one of his hands wrought in the work, and with other hand held a weapon."*

18; *"For the builders, everyone had his sword girded by his side, and so builded. And he that sounded the trumpet was by me."*

A good leader is able to design strategies that produce resource. Nehemiah's creativity kept the enemies from invading the children of Israel while they were working on the walls.

6. Courage: Bravery, valor, boldness, strength, enduring, heroism, defiance, strong-minded, keeping your chin up.

Nehemiah showed courage when he asked the king for a twelve-year leave of absence.
Nehemiah 2:5; *"And I said unto the king, if it please the king, and if thy servant have found favor in thy sight, that thou wouldest send me unto Judah, unto the city of my fathers' sepulchers, that I may build it."*

6; *"And the king said unto me, (the queen also sitting by him,) for how long shall thy journey be? And when wilt thou return? So it pleased the king to send me; and I set him a time."*

Nehemiah 5:14; *"Moreover from the time that I was appointed to be their governor in the land of Judah, from the twentieth year even unto the two and thirtieth year of Anaxerxes the king, that is twelve years, I and my brethren have not eaten the bread of the governor."*

Nehemiah showed courage when he responded to the enemy attacks.

Notice **Nehemiah 4:14;** *"And I looked, and rose up, and said unto the nobles, and to the rulers, and to the rest of the people. Be not ye afraid of them: remember the Lord, which is great and terrible, and fight for your brethren, your sons, and your daughters, your wives, and your houses."*

Nehemiah 5:7-13

7; "Then I consulted with myself, and I rebuked the nobles, and the rulers, and said unto them, Ye exact usury, every one of his brother. And I set a great assembly against them."

8; "And I said unto them, we after our ability have redeemed our brethren the Jews, which were sold unto the heathen; and will ye even sell your brethren? Or shall they be sold unto us? Then held they their peace, and found nothing to answer."

9; Also I said, it is not good that ye do: ought ye not to walk in the fear of our God because of the reproach of the heathen our enemies?"

10; "I likewise, and my brethren, and my servants, might exact of them money and corn: I pray you, let us leave off this usury."

11; "Restore, I pray you, to them, even this day, their lands, their vineyards, their olive yards, and their houses, also the hundredth part of the money, and of the corn, the wine, and the oil, that ye exact of them,"

12; "Then said they, we will restore them, and will require nothing of them; so will we do as thou sayest. Then I called the priests, and took an oath of them, that they should do according to this promise."

13; " Also I shook my lap, and said, So God shake out every man from his house, and from his labor, that performeth not this promise, even thus be he shaken out, and emptied. And the entire congregation said, Amen, and praised the Lord. And the people did according to this promise."
Courage is not the absence of fear, it is moving ahead in spite of your fear.

7. <u>Clear Conscience</u>: Nehemiah was a man of integrity, wholesomeness, oneness, and righteousness. Nehemiah had a clear conscience in business. He did not abuse his position, power, or privilege as a leader, even though he could have.

Notice Nehemiah 5:14-19
14; *"Moreover from the time that I was appointed to be their governor in the land of Judah, from the twentieth year even unto the two and thirtieth year of Artaxerxes the king, that is, twelve years, I and my brethren have not eaten the bread of the governor."*

15; *"But the former governors that had been before me were chargeable unto the people, and had taken of them bread and wine, beside forty shekels of silver; yea, even their servants bare rule over the people: but so did not I, because of the fear of God."*

16; *"Yea, also I continued in the work of this wall, neither bought we any land: and all my servants were gathered thither unto the work."*

17; *"Moreover there were at my table a hundred and fifty of the Jews and rulers, beside those that came unto us from among the heathen that are about us."*

18; *"Now that which was prepared for me daily was one ox and six choice sheep; also fowls were prepared for me, and once in ten days store of all sorts of wine: yet for all this required not I the bread of the governor, because the bondage was heavy upon this people."*

19; *"Think upon me, my God, for good, according to all that I have done for this people."*

He always used good judgment of right and wrong. He was sensible. He had a good understanding. He was aware of what was going on and he was still able to reason and make good judgment. To be a good leader you must have a clear conscience.

8. <u>**Conviction:**</u> *Strong belief. For he that cometh to God must believe that he is and that he is a rewarder of them that diligently seek him. Faith means that we believe God to be absolutely trustworthy. For the Psalmist in Psalms 121:3-5 put it this way.*

3; *"He will not suffer thy foot to be moved: He that keepeth thee will not slumber."*
4; *"Behold, he that keepeth Israel shall neither slumber nor sleep."*
5; *"The Lord is thy keeper: the Lord is thy shade upon thy right hand."*

The lifestyle of a leader will either make him, or break him. If he neglects the cultivation of humility and faith, he is in big trouble. On the other hand, if any one sets himself to be God's kind of man, by God's grace, you can be the man God wants you to be

2 Chronicles 16:9; *"For the eyes of the Lord run to and fro throughout the whole earth, to show himself strong in the behalf of them whose heart is perfect toward him. Herein thou hast done foolishly: therefore from henceforth thou shalt have wars."*

CHAPTER 8

The Spiritual Lifestyle of a Leader

The primary characteristics exhibited by leaders should be purity of life.
Daniel 1:8; *"But Daniel purposed in his heart that he would not defile himself with the portion of the king's meat, nor with the wine which he drank: therefore he requested of the prince of the eunuchs that he might not defile himself."*

The apostle continued his theme.

2 Corinthians 6:14; *"Be ye not unequally yoke together with unbelievers; for what fellowship hath righteous with unrighteousness? And what communion hath light with darkness?"*

15; *"And what concord hath Christ with Belial? Or what part hath he that believeth with an infidel?"*

16; *"And what agreement hath the temple of God with idols? For ye are the temple of the living God; as God hath said, I will DWELL IN THEM, AND WALK IN THEM; AND I WILL BE THEIR GOD, AND THEY SHALL BE MY PEOPLE."*

Paul used the five questions just quoted to draw a line of boundaries between God and the opposition. On one side, he gathers righteousness, light, Christ, faith, and the house of God. On the other side, he lists lawlessness, darkness, Satan, unbelief, and false worship. He states that you cannot mix these two lists.

A leader must choose to live on one side, or the other. Leroy Elms states in his book, *"Be the leader you were meant to be."* The leader must set an example in his behavior according to the standards of the scriptures.

Paul says in *1 Timothy 3:2;* *"A bishop them must be blameless, the husband of one wife, viligant, sober, of good behavior, given to hospitality, apt to teach;"*

1 Samuel 16:7; *"But the Lord said unto Samuel, Look not on his countenance, or on the height of his stature; because I have refused him: for the Lord seeth not as man seeth; for man looketh on the outward appearance, but the Lord looketh on the heart."*

2 Timothy 2:19; *"Nevertheless the foundation of God standeth sure, having this seal, The Lord knoweth them that are his. And, let every one that nameth the name of Christ depart from iniquity."*

20; *"But in a great house there are not only vessels of gold and some silver, but also of wood and of earth; and some to honor, and some to dishonor."*

21; *"If a man therefore purge himself from these, he shall be vessel unto honor, sanctified, and meet for the master's use and prepared unto every good work."*

The simple spiritual truth is that a man can choose which kind of vessel he will be in the household of God. It's his choice to be a vessel of honor or dishonor. God is looking for a life that is clean and pure. Only then that life will be a vessel unto honor, sanctified and meet for the master's use. Perfected unto every good work.

God has promised to show Himself to others through His leaders.

Ezekiel 36:23; *"And I will sanctify my great name, which was profaned among the heathen, which ye have profaned in the midst of them; and the heathen shall know that I am the Lord, saith the Lord God, when I shall be sanctified in you before their eyes."*

A leader must ask himself the following questions and examine himself to see how this is applied to his life:

1. Is what I'm doing helpful?

Paul says in ***1 Corinthians 6:12***; *"All things are lawful unto me, but all things are not expedient; all things are lawful for me, but I will not be brought under the power of any,"*

Is what you are about to do helpful or harmful to you and others, physically? Will it help you mentally or corrupt your mind? Will it help you grow or stagnate your spiritual development?

2. Will it cause others to fail?

Paul says in ***1 Corinthians 8:12***; *"But when ye sin so against the brethren, and wound their weak conscience, ye sin against Christ."*

13; *"Wherefore, if meat make my brother to offend, I will eat no flesh while the world standeth, lest I make my brother to offend."*

Will what I am doing, cause others to fail? Maybe I can handle it, but will it affect those who are watching me? Will my actions cause them problems? Will my accusations lead them into trouble? Therefore, a leader must think of others when he decides his activities.

The things I do will enslave me. Notice what Paul says in ***1 Corinthians 6:12***; *"All things are lawful unto me, but all things are not expedient; all things are lawful for me, but I will not be brought under the power of any."*

I know many people today; some are family members who are slaves to cigarettes, liquor, drugs, and immorality. Do the things I do, glorify God?

Notice what Paul said in ***1 Corinthians 10:31***; *"Whether therefore ye eat, or drink, or whatsoever ye do, do all to the glory of God."*

The answer: "Man's chief end is to glorify God, and to enjoy Him forever. Leaders must ask themselves this question: Do the things I do glorify God?"

Another spiritual characteristic of leadership is humility (state of being humble). A humble spirit is a mark of one God uses.

God requires a humble spirit in his servants. Notice **Isaiah 42:8**; *"I am the Lord: that is my name: and my glory will not give to another, neither my praise to graven images."*

God resists the proud, He does not bless them.

Notice **1 Peter 5:5-6**

5; *"Likewise, ye younger, submit yourselves unto the elders. Yea, all of you be subject one to another, and be clothed with humility: for GOD RESISTETH THE PROUD, AND GIVETH GRACE TO THE HUMBLE."*

6; *"Humble yourselves therefore under the mighty hand of God, that he may exalt you in due time;"*

Many passages of scripture deal with this subject. Here are some practical ones:

Micah 6:8; *"He hath showed thee, O man, what is good; and what doth the Lord require of thee, but do justly, and to love mercy, and to walk humbly with thy God?"*

Proverbs 6:16; *"These six things doth the Lord hate: yea, seven are an abomination unto him."*

17; *"A proud look, a lying tongue, and hands that shed innocent blood."*

18; *"A heart that deviseth wicked imaginations, feet that be swift in running to mischief."*

19; *"A false witness that speaketh lies, and he that soweth discord among brethren."*

Philippians 2:3; *"Let nothing be done through strife or vainglory; but in lowliness of mind let each esteem other better than themselves."*

4; *"Look not every man on his own things, but every man also on the things of others."*

Some leaders will prosper only as he walks in the spirit of humility. It has been observed in the life of men in positions of leadership and it has been tragic to watch their spiritual leadership decline, where humility was not practiced.

A good example of how pride can affect a leader is found in **2 Chronicles 26** (read in its entirety), but notice verse 16, *"But when he was strong, his heart was lifted up to his destruction: for he transgressed against the Lord his God, and went into the temple of the Lord to burn incense upon the altar of incense."*

Pride is the greatest enemy in any leaders' life. Leroy Elms says in his book, *"Be the leader you were meant to be."* When a man is full of pride he cannot see the best way of achieving his purpose. For he only see the way that brings him the most honor and acclaim. He sees only what his pride want him to see. King Nebuchadnezzar fell because of it.

Daniel 5: 20; *"But when his heart was lifted up, and his mind hardened in pride, he was deposed from his kingly throne, and they took is glory from him;"*

A proud spirit is deadly to a leader, it will kill his effectiveness for God, and it breeds two dreadful diseases of the soul. Pride makes a man <u>self-sufficient</u> and <u>unteachable</u>, it will bind him to his own needs. It will also, ignore the good advice and counsel of others.

Notice **Proverbs 15:22**; *"Without counsel purposes are disappointed: but in the multitude of counselors they are established."*

A leader must be teachable, but not gullible, and he must weigh the counsel he receives in the light of the Bible and the welfare of the church.

Proverbs 11:14; *"Where no counsel is, the people fall: but in the multitude of counselors there is safety."*

Secondly, insecurity, the fear of failure brings everything to a standstill; rather than admit his weakness and step out in faith, he does nothing.

How does a leader maintain a humble spirit before the Lord? Many things are involved of course, but one stands out. If the leader lives in that spirit of praise he will be reminded of his own sinfulness and weakness. It will come from the heart, which is filled with praises of God for his holiness and power. Notice what Paul says in **Philippians 4:13**; *"I can do all things through Christ, which strengthen me."*

Faith is a vital characteristic in the lifestyle of the leader. Notice **Hebrew 11:6**; *"But without faith it is impossible to please him: for he cometh to God must believe that he is, and that he is a rewarder of them that diligently seek him."*

The Psalmist puts it this way.

Psalms 121:3; *"He will not suffer thy foot to be moved: he that keepeth thee will not slumber."*

4; "Behold, he that keepeth Israel shall neither slumber nor sleep."

5; "The Lord is thy keeper: the Lord is thy shade upon thy right hand."

By God's grace, you can be the man or woman God wants you to be.

CHAPTER 9

What Followers are Expecting from Leaders

My informal survey on what followers expect from leaders: secular and spiritual. I am focusing mostly on spiritual leaders and the result of the overwhelming two-month survey of approximately 120 people.

The first thing a follower wants to see in a leader is character. More than anything else, followers want to believe that their leaders are ethical and honest. Most want to say, "One day, some day, I want to be like him or her."

They also look for these three qualities in leaders:

1. **<u>Goodness:</u>** The ability to do what is good and beneficial to others (not selfish).
2. **<u>Righteousness:</u>** Doing what is right in all relationships.
3. **<u>Truth:</u>** The expression of your spirit; open, honest, full of integrity.

In his: "In Joy Life" seminar, Dr. John Maxwell said; followers should ask their leaders the following question:

1. Is this for the glory of God or your own?
2. Is this for the best in me or in others?
3. The decisions you make, will they hold up to scrutiny?
4. What would Jesus do, if He had to make this decision?

Texas business Editor-in-Chief Bruce Austin, said, *"We have been programmed to acquire at the expense of both our personal integrity and our personal fulfillment."*

The survey also revealed that followers want to sense competency from their leader; competent, rightfully belonging and qualified or capable.

"Getting to the Top", USA Today executives polled the most important skills to get to the top.

1. 15% Ambition
2. 6%   Competency
3. 6%   Intelligence
4. 6%   Personality
5. 3%   Politics
6. 2%   Luck Timing
7. 1%   Nepotism

According to Dr. John Maxwell "In Joy Life" seminar (1990), "What the church never taught me."

1. The ability to bounce back; which is attitude.
2. The ability to influence people; that's leadership skill.
3. The ability to relate well with people; that's people skill.
4. The ability to develop people; that's equipping skill.

The level of competence is the ability to see what needs to happen, and the ability to make it happen. A sign on an optometrist's office reads: "IF YOU DON'T SEE WHAT YOU WANT, YOU'VE COME TO THE RIGHT PLACE."

Followers want to be challenged by their leaders. I have been trying all my life, first, to visualize for me; second, have others to visualize for me; third, to get others to see with me. To succeed in business, it is vital to help people to visualize as you. Seeing was the objective in the broadest sense, "I am visionary,"

Leaders should create a clear compelling vision that, will give others a reason to contribute to the cause.

Habakkuh 2:2; "*And the Lord answered me, and said, Write the vision, and make it plan upon tables, that he may run that readeth it.*"

3; "*For the vision is yet for an appointed time, but at the end it shall speak, and not lie: though it tarry, wait for it; because it will surely come, it will not tarry.*"

Five Things That Will Limit A Leaders Vision:
1. When more time is spent on problems, than leading.
2. When you are too busy to lead, because your calendar is filled with the important things.
3. When you spend more time remembering the past, than you do preparing for the future.
4. When you become more concerned with the people you have, that you don't want anymore.
5. When you spend too much time and energy attempting to recover inactive people.

It's easier to get people to do what they want to do, than to get them to do what you want them to do. Leaders should maintain a high personal integrity in decision making.

1. God
2. People
3. Leadership

"Strong convictions precede great actions; let him who would move and convinced others, be moved and convinced himself," J.F. Clarke

"What convinces is conviction, believe in the argument you are advancing; if you don't you are as good as dead; the other people will sense that something isn't there, and no chain of reasoning, no matter how logical, or elegant, or brilliant, will win your case for you," Lyndon B. Johnson.

To Recap:

1. Followers want to see <u>character</u> in their leaders.
2. Followers want to sense <u>competence</u> in their leaders.
3. Followers want to be <u>challenged</u> by their leaders.
4. Followers want to feel <u>conviction</u> from their leaders.
5. Followers want to make a <u>contribution</u> with their leaders.

"No individual has any right to come into the world, and go out of it, without leaving behind him, distinct and legitimate reason for having passed through it," Elliott Lawrence, George Washington.

The leader's responsibility is to help people find their purpose. When a leader practices good leadership, they will enable people to use their own initiative and experience, toward accomplishing their vision.

"The prospects never looked brighter and the problems never looked tougher. Anyone who isn't stirred by both of these statements, is too tired to be of much use in the days ahead," John W. Gardner, former Secretary of Health, Education and Welfare.

I have often had other pastors ask me, "What motivates me to continue to work as hard as I do?" To keep up with this awesome job and responsibility as a minister of God; I reply, "I have dreamed a dream that's bigger than me; and that dream allows me at any time, at any moment, to give up all that I am; in order to receive all that I can become." Therefore, I have to trust God's resources, since the dream is bigger than all my abilities and acquaintances. My dream is a promise of what I shall be one day. Yes, I have a dream; it's a God-given dream; it's greater than any of my gifts, it's as large as the world; but it begins with one. Will you join me?

NOTES

CHAPTER 10

People Skills How to Cultivate Good Relationships

The effectiveness of a leader's relationships is determined by his ability to relate to others. Leadership is influence; whether it's effective (positive) influence, power to influence; <u>what they say</u>, <u>what they think</u>, and <u>what they do</u>; it influences those who follow them. There are three components in relational leadership found in *John 10:3-5.*

John 10:3; "To him the porter openeth; and the sheep hear his voice: and he calleth his own sheep by name, and leadeth them out."

4; "And when he putteth forth his own sheep, he goeth before them, and the sheep follow him: for they know his voice."

5; "And a stranger will they not follow, but will flee from him: for they know not the voice of strangers."

I: The shepherd knows his sheep intimately, verse 3.
   1. He recognizes them instantly.
   2. The sheep knows his voice.
   3. He knows their names.
   4. He is personally acquainted with each sheep.

II: Relationships are built on trust, verse 4.
   1. The sheep know their leader (some leaders are not transparent,)
   2. The sheep hear his voice and come to him.
   3. They will run from a stranger.
   4. Leaders must be worthy of their followers trust.

III: Relationships are modeled.
   1. The shepherd walks ahead of his sheep.

A leader should know how to handle conflicts. There is a principle that is used in the secular world; for managers, presidents, and corporate owners. This principle is called "101 Principle." If you are a church leader and one of your followers is difficult to get along with, you find the 1% which the two of you can agree on, then give 100% of your efforts and abilities toward that one thing. Then, and only then, you stand a good chance of winning him or her. That's what Jesus did.

Luke 15:4; *"What man of you, having a hundred sheep, if he lose one of them, doth not leave the ninety and nine in the wilderness, and go after that which is lost, until he find it?"*

5; "And when he hath found it, he layeth it on his shoulders, rejoicing."

6; "And when he cometh home, he calleth together his friends and neighbors, saying unto them, rejoice with me; for I have found my sheep which was lost."

He left the 99 and went after the one that was lost.

The following are ten ways a leader can develop his people skills in handling conflicts according to Rick Warren at "The Encouraging Word Ministry" seminar.

1. <u>***Use the 101 Principle***</u>
   Follow the 101 principle, try to find one thing you can agree on with the difficult person and then give it 100%.

2. <u>***Love People***</u>
   Love people more than opinions; don't let your opinions destroy your relationships. Highly opinionated people normally don't make good leaders.

3. <u>***Give Others the Benefit of the Doubt***</u>
   We usually rule ourselves with our hearts, but somehow we tend to rule others with our mouths. If you want to enhance your people skills in this area, just reverse the rule.

Matthew 7:12; *"Therefore all things whatsoever ye would that men should do to you, do even so to them: for this is the law and prophets."*

4. <u>***Learn to be Flexible***</u>
   Thomas Jefferson once said, <u>***"In matters of principle, stand like a rock, in matters of taste, swim with the current."***</u> Good leaders know how to say, "I am sorry" quicker than followers. Effective leaders know how to back down, they don't constantly feel the need to defend their right; they learn to be flexible.

5. *<u>Providing an Escape</u>*
Provide an escape hatch for the person in conflict. It takes a good-hearted person to allow someone who has been defeated, to ease out of a situation and be able to save their face. **<u>Leaders, once you have made your point, back off, and spare the person.</u>**

6. *<u>Keeping your Attitudes in Check</u>*
Check your own attitudes. Wrong attitudes will cause relational conflicts. If you are having conflicts with several people about the same matter; then it's a good chance the problem is you. The attitude that you project towards others will determine how they feel about you.

7. *<u>Overreacting to Conflicts</u>*
Don't overreact to conflicts; don't drop a bomb when a slingshot will work. If you expect conflicts, you must be prepared to handle them.

8. *<u>Becoming Defenseless</u>*
Don't become defensive. You will never win a relationship when you are defensive. A secure leader knows how to say "I was wrong or I misunderstood you, please forgive me." We never resolve differences by being defensive.

9. *<u>Welcome the Conflicts</u>*
Make it a learning experience. Conflicts will give you ulcers or understanding. Remember **Proverbs 3:5**; *"Trust in the Lord with all thine heart; and lean not unto thine own understanding."*

10. *<u>Take a Risk</u>*
Take a risk and extend your hand out first, as a gesture of friendship. Many people fail to solve problems because they are afraid to take risks that may embarrass them. Leaders are always going to be hurt over something. People are not going to always love you. Let's look at how to use people skills to cultivate a relationship.

John 10:3; *"To him the porter openeth; and the sheep hear his voice: and he calleth his own sheep by name, and leadeth them out."*

4; *"And when he putteth forth his own sheep, he goeth before them, and the sheep follow him: for they know his voice."*

5; *"And a stranger will they not follow, but will flee from him: for they know not the voice of strangers."*

Here we find seven components to cultivate good relationships:

1. <u>*Know them – this is the beginning of effective relationship.*</u>
   Acknowledge your need for others, and then you must admit your needs to others. A complete Christian is filled with God's spirit, but is also surrounded by gifted friends. Until you acknowledge your needs to your friends, you will never cultivate effective relationships.

2. <u>*Learn to believe in the value of others.*</u>
   "A great man shows his greatness by how he treats the little man."

3. <u>*Determine whether you are a motivator or a manipulator.*</u>
   Motivation is moving together for his or her mutual advantage. Manipulation is moving together for his or her advantage. Everybody wins with a motivator. Only the leader wins with a manipulator.

4. <u>*Concentrate on people, not the problem.*</u>
   The only thing God is going to rescue from this planet is people. If you have a ministry of performance, you must build into the life of others. Some of the most miserable people are program changers and builders; but some of the happiest people are people changers.

5. <u>*Grow them.*</u>
   If you want people to grow, then you must be available for them when they need you. Be a reliable leader. Relationships grown on consistency shrink on moodiness. Learn how to be approachable. Everybody likes to be around people who entrust us, teach us, and help us to grow.

6. <u>*Show them.*</u>
   People do what they see their leaders model. People don't care how much you know, until they know how much you care. <u>**They know how much you care by the way you act toward them,**</u> not by what you say.

7. <u>*Leaders should spend three-quarters of their time with people. Why?*</u>
   A. The largest single cost in most business is people.
   B. The most valuable asset of any business is its people.

C. All plans are carried out, or fail to be carried out by people.
D. Your relationships with people will determine the success of your leadership. We can either be a plow type leader; that means to cultivate them, or a bulldozer; that means to destroy them. If all leaders would learn some people skills, what a great world this would be.

NOTES

NOTES

CHAPTER 11

Transformational Leadership

Since the publication of James McGregor Burns' book, Leadership, in 1978, viewing the leader as transformational rather than transactional became the focus of a great amount of leadership research. Rather than exchanging reward for achieved goals, transformational leadership is a comprehensive approach that strives to change or transform followers to transcend their own short-term needs for their longer-term self-development, the good of the group, the organization, and society. It is a lofty goal.

Burns (1978) believed that leaders were either transactional or transformational. You were either one or the other, and transformational was better. However, seven years later Bernard Bass (1985) proposed that both types of leadership are necessary and that transformational leadership actually enhances transactional behaviors. Since then, researchers have described the hybrid nature of leadership in many of the nation's great leaders. A transformation leader is likely the kind of leader most people have in mind today when they think of an ideal leader. Transformational leadership models generally include four factors that are concerned with transforming behaviors, plus the two factors that involve transactional exchanges:

Transformational Factors:

1. *Charisma* or idealized influence.
   Leaders are strong role model and inspire others want to follow their vision.

2. *Inspirational Motivation.*
   Leaders communicate high expectations and use emotional appeals.

3. *Intellectual Stimulation.*
   Leaders challenge followers to develop innovative ways of problem solving.

4. *Individualized Consideration.*
Leaders pay attention to individual needs and assign meaningful projects to help followers grow personally.

Transactional Factors:

5. *Contingent Reward.*
Leaders negotiate with followers about what needs to be done and the reward for meeting the goal (positive reinforcement).

6. *Management-by-Exception.*
Leaders monitor followers and provide corrective criticism if standards are not met (essentially negative reinforcement).

Transformational leadership links leaders and followers more than previous theories, and seeks to raise the level of motivation and morality in both. This relatively new leadership paradigm at best sees followers converted into leaders, and at worst, could be abused by changing people's values in a wrong direction. Overall, however, transformational leadership provides a way to motivate followers toward achievement and self-actualization instead of security, and provides opportunity for more comprehensive organizational change. The Multifactor Leadership Questionnaire (MLQ) Form 6S (Bass & Avolio, 1992) helps determine the leader's strengths and weaknesses in transformational leadership.

Implications for Church Leadership

Transformational leadership has extraordinary appeal to church leaders who consider themselves to be in the transformational business. Pastors and church leaders consider the church a place of pastoral and corporate transformation, thus the term itself has great currency with church leaders. Church leaders hope to rise up other leaders and a "multiplication mentality" pervades many Christian ministries (2 Timothy 2:2). For the church, transformational leadership promotes the leadership process from a mere exchange of rewards-for-service toward a transformed and transforming community of individuals. Some of the implications of the transformational leadership model for the church may be:

1. Church leaders should seek supernatural charisma from God. In church the "charisma" of transformation leadership is often connected with anointing or "unction" from God. That is, church people often recognize a spiritual authority in some leaders that is supernatural and God-given, and more than personality. The effective church leader ought to seek this supernatural charisma if they wish to be a transformational leader. In Christian thinking God sometimes grants anointing, unction, or gifts to whom He

pleases, but at other times He does so in response to a person's seeking of His gifts. Church leaders ought to seek whatever supernatural gifts from God that would enhance transforming the people.

2. Great church leaders should not shy away from casting high expectations for their people and from making highly emotional appeals-this is a portion of transformational leadership. In local churches, such behavior is exhibited in preaching. It is possible to be a transformational leader without access to the pulpit, but it is harder.

3. Transformational leaders should equip their people to think out of the (traditional) box. While transformational leaders think creatively themselves, they also encourage their people to develop this habit as well. It isn't hard to find pastors who think outside the box. However, pastors who enable their people to do so are harder to find. In many churches, the pastor does most of the creative thinking in order to develop a solution. Only rarely does the pastor intellectually stimulate the people to enable them to become out-of-the-box thinkers so that pastor can trust the problem to the people. Then he could watch them develop their own creative and innovate solutions.

4. Church leaders should regularly enter a process of self-examination to ponder their personal motivation, seeking God to cleanse the elements of motivation that issue from a desire to build a great ministerial career, great personal kingdom, or become famous. Dying out to such motivations can permit higher level of motivation to emerge. This will enable a minister to succeed not just in the people's eyes, but also in God's. An effective church leader in God's sight will have positive expressions of affiliation, achievement, and power, using altruistic values to avoid developing a personal career path, or seeking to develop fame among ministerial peers.

5. Self-assessment is the beginning of the three-step process for re-creating an organization with positive ethical motivations. Beginning with the primary leader, the entire collection of leaders – ministerial and lay – can move the inner motivations for leading from the negative affiliation, achievement, and power motivations to altruistic, positive, and ethical motivations.

NOTES

CHAPTER 12

Organizational Culture and Leadership

Edgar Schein defines <u>organizational culture</u> as the "pattern of shared basic assumptions that the group learned as it solved its problems of external adaptation and internal integration that has worked well enough to be considered valid therefore, to be taught to new members as the correct way to perceive, think, and feel in relation to these problems". Schein recommends analyzing organizational culture on three levels, in order to understand the embedded sources of the values and actions commonly seen in an organization.

Levels of Organizational Culture (Schein, 1992)
<u>*Artifacts*</u> – visible organizational structures and processes (hard to decipher meaning)
<u>*Espoused Values*</u> – strategies, goals, philosophies (includes justifications for behavior)
<u>*Basic Underlying Assumptions*</u> – unconscious, taken-for-granted beliefs, perceptions, thoughts, and feelings (ultimate sources of values and actions)

Each level affects the other levels. This interconnected sets of values identified as the preferred (or obligatory) state of behavior within the organization is sometimes called an ideology. An ideology is a deeper level than the espoused values and norms (specific expectations) and the public identity of an organization.

<u>*Not every collection of people develops a culture.*</u> Since organizations are most effective when the members share values, leaders need to see organizational culture as a valuable resource to manage. As for influencing cultural change, Mainero and Tromley (1989) believe that behavior affect values and suggest five ways courageous leaders attempt to change culture.

Intervention Points for Influencing Organizational Culture

1) Behavioral change (requiring compliance to new routines, with the belief that values and beliefs will follow)
2) Justification for behavior (members seeing inherent worth in new behavior)
3) Cultural communication to motivate new behavior (memos, rituals, stories, dress)
4) Socialization of new members (or hire one who fit with culture)

5) Removal of members who deviate from the culture (weeding out cultural misfits, after careful diagnosis)

Founding leaders are able over time to embed their basic assumptions in the patterns of the group, and therefore help create the organizational culture. However, if a leader sets out to change the existing culture of an organization, they can expect it to be difficult, time consuming, and highly anxiety provoking. Yet, leaders are sometimes able to get at the deeper levels of how cultural assumptions were made, and deal with any dysfunction at that level. This must include the leaders revealing assumptions within themselves, and a willingness to absorb the anxiety and risk produced by such a challenge in the organization.

Implications for Church Leadership

The church is not merely a collection of people in a human organization but a spiritual organism under the influence of the Holy Spirit. The Bible and theology lay out clear underlying assumptions about the church – this is called our ecclesiology. The Bible should provide common values for the church. These underlying (and perhaps never-stated) assumptions and publicly declared values should then produce the artifacts of our present-day structure and systems in the church. We share many underlying assumptions and values across denominational and theological lines, however, the artifacts may differ widely. Church leaders should be keen on understanding organizational culture, for one of our tasks is to cultivate a common culture in the church based on common values and assumptions. Indeed, one of the purposes of preaching is to "get the church on the same page" concerning values and assumptions. Some of the implications for church leadership from the research in organizational culture may be:

1. Pastors often attempt to change the artifacts (the structures, programs, and processes) without addressing the espoused values and underlying assumptions first. Such surfaces changing seldom works. Changing the people's underlying assumptions and espoused values may take longer than merely changing a program or process, but it leads to more permanent change in a congregation.

2. Due to a series of program-pastors, some churches have hardly any common ground in values or assumptions. These churches need long-term teaching, preaching, and discipling to bring the group to collective common values and assumptions. Until then such a people may have no more in common than a random crowd attending a movie theater – they come because they like the show but have nothing else in common. A leader's job in such a church is to develop an organizational culture based on solid biblical and theological foundations. Preaching is the primary pathway to such commonality.

3. Mainero and Tromley, however, offer a counterpoint to the above. They raise a point often debated in the church: do we change people's minds first, expecting them to thus change their behavior; or can we start by changing their behavior first, then leading them to the underlying values and beliefs? Mainero and Tromley suggest we can start at the behavioral end (e.g., starting outreach teams instead of just preaching on evangelism) before the people are even convinced in their minds of that value. Then, as the people act in new ways, their values and assumptions will catch up to their behavior.

"Culture Trumps Vision" by, Dr. Sam Chand

Many pastors pour time and resources into communicating a strong, clear vision for their church, but when their vision fails to materialize, they become confused and frustrated. Quite often, they don't realize that culture-not-vision is the most powerful factor in any organization. It's often unspoken, unexamined, and unnoticed, but it determines how people respond to leadership and vision. My book, *CRACKING THE CHURCH'S CULTURE CODE: Seven Keys to Unleashing Vision & Inspiration*, describes the concept of organizational culture in a church environment, outlines the impact of culture, and offers the promise that the reader will be able to recognize the connection between culture and vision, empower people to do their very best and love doing it, and have a clear process to implement cultural change.

As a leadership consultant, I often wondered why the best strategic plans and good leadership were not able to move churches in the desired direction. Then I saw and smelled the noxious carbon monoxide of organizations-toxic culture. Quite often, leaders don't see or smell it, but it poisons their relationships and derails their vision.

Churches have a wide range of personalities. A few common traits characterize healthy church cultures, and a set of opposite traits is found in unhealthy ones. Leaders all along the spectrum long for their churches to be strong, healthy environments where people thrive, support each other, and celebrate each other's successes.

Some comments I hear from church leaders are, "We spent time and money to re-energize the congregation. We took our top staff on a retreat to instill the new vision into them. We hired more staff, and we reformatted our worship experience. We started new programs. We redesigned our stage set. We created a killer website, reconfigured our offices, redecorated to create a fresh ambiance, and designed a new logo for the church. We even wrote a song about how great we are! But none of this has made a bit of difference. We haven't gone backward, and I'm glad of that, but I thought we'd be way ahead of where we are today. What am I missing?"

Toxic culture is like carbon monoxide: you don't see or smell it but you wake up dead! Senior pastors do a lot of good things, but they fail to understand the impact of the existing organizational culture on their new, exciting vision for the church. It is like changing the engine on a sports car to make it faster, but it's spinning its wheels in the mud. Or to use a different metaphor, they try to transplant a heart into a patient whose body rejected the foreign organ. No matter how perfect the new heart is, the patient had no chance at all unless the body accepted it.

Culture not vision or strategy – is the most powerful factor in any organization. It determines the receptivity of staff and volunteers to new ideas, unleashes or dampens creativity, builds or erodes enthusiasm, and creates a sense of pride or deep discouragement about working or being involved there.

How much does the average staff member feel he or she has input the direction and strategy of the church?

Who has the ear of the top leaders? How did these people win a hearing with the leaders?

Who is rewarded, and for what accomplishments?

What is the level of loyalty up and down the organizational chart?

How are decisions made, deferred, denied or delayed?

Who are the non-positional power brokers?

Where are control problems and power are struggles most evident?

How is "turf" defined and protected?

I encourage you to form an informal team of key staff and/or volunteer leaders with the senior pastor and have an honest conversation about these questions on the topic of culture. You'll be glad you did.

NOTES

CHAPTER 13

Organizational Change Theory

Organizational change is a generalized term for organizational development (OD) and organizational transformation (OT) theory and practice. The theory and practice of OD deals with planned change efforts in managing the human dynamics in an organization. These "first order" changes include staff training and other continuous improvement strategies. OT addresses more massive changes in structures, processes, culture, and dealing with an external environment. This is often unplanned, radical, and revolutionary to the organization's structures. Leaders who initiate and/or manage organizational change efforts intend to improve organizational effectiveness and individual well-being. Three theorists are notable in the field and important for leaders to know when understanding organizational change.

<u>*LEWIN's (1947) Three- Step Procedure*</u> is a result of four years of studies and action research designed to change food habits in line with war needs during WWII. Since Lewin believed that all human systems attempt to maintain equilibrium that provides predictability and meaning, he concluded that all change processes needed to follow this procedure:

1. *Unfreezing* – sufficient discomfort creating motivation concerning new goals, and psychological safety to develop readiness to change.
2. *Moving/changing* - cognitive restructuring; includes demonstrations, training, and empowerment.
3. *Refreezing* – applying reinforcement and feedback; often includes new rewards for desired behavior, and new accountability measures to help establish the new level of behavior.

At the heart of this classic theory are the principles that enable people to unlearn old behaviors (cognitive change) and learn new ones (behavioral change).

<u>*TICHY's (1983) Technical, Political, Cultural Framework*</u> (TPC) uses the metaphor of a strategic three-strand rope to stress the importance of overarching, inter-related systems that cut across the other components that affect the organization: The three strands are:

1. *Technical* – based on hard data, representing rational perspective.
2. *Political* – based on power dynamics between individuals and groups.
3. *Cultural* – based on shared values and norms.

All three of these systems must be aligned with each other and with any one "change lever" in an organization for change to be effective. Change levers are the individual components of an organization, such as mission, strategy, interest groups, task, formal structures, people, processes, informal networks, and environment. TPC places strong emphasis on effective leadership as essential to change, since it is perceived to pervade the whole organizational framework.

<u>**GLADWELL's (2000) book, The Tipping Point**</u> provides an appropriate description of how change happens "virally" and <u>seldom happens as planned</u>. It can be explained by the following three characteristics:

1. *Contagiousness* – the word-of-mouth spreading of the fame/notoriety of a product or event.
2. *Small causes can have big effects* – little changes can have large consequences.
3. *Change happens suddenly* – the notion of reaching critical mass, when the virus has spread sufficiently, it seems the whole world is instantly aware of the phenomenon.

Gladwell argues that this kind of change happens because of the following three primary components:

a) "The Law of the Few" says there are three kinds of influential people in an organization: connectors – infectious people with personality-based strengths to spread the word, mavens- collectors of information, and salesmen – persuaders that relate, empathize, and influence.
b) The content of the message and its "stickiness factor" constantly refined for maximum effect.
c) The context/environment in which the infection occurs.

Implications for Church Leadership

Most church leaders assume things need changing. Indeed, the notion of the kingdom of God growing like a mustard plant or spreading through the whole lump of dough like yeast assumes change. In some sense all Christians are change-agents. The world is out of sync with God's will and Christians are in the work of helping God bring it back into alignment – "thy kingdom come" (Matthew 6). While everything does not have to be changed, leaders are called to change the things that need changing (and have the wisdom to know what needs changing and what should be left alone.) Most church leaders assume it is their responsibility to understand from God's leading what changes should be made. Therefore, organizational change theory is relevant to pastors since it speaks to how to effect these changes. Some implications from organizational change theory for church leadership may be:

1). Changing often occurs in stages, beginning with Lewin's process of unfreezing-preparing for change to occur. This role is similar to John the Baptist's work, but it is often not as popular with pastors. But forcing change without the proper preparation may backfire in a church organization and result in unintended consequences – perhaps the changing of the pastor.

2). Tichy's three-strand rope implies that change is not one-dimensional; rather it includes at least three inter-related systems. Church leaders are often better equipped to outline the technical-rational arguments for change than they are to understand the political-power dynamics and the cultural-shared values elements. <u>Church leaders should be skilled at working with all three strands.</u>

3). Gladwell's "tipping point" concept helps church leaders understand how sometimes change strikes like lightning rather than coming in a measured, incremental process. Sometimes after a long period of trying to change, a massive shift just happens so swiftly that the church launches forward, skipping several decades of what would have been incremental change.

NOTES

NOTES

CHAPTER 14

Who is Qualified to Lead?

All of the leadership principles in this dissertation will be extrapolations from Biblical scriptures of biblical principles (KJV). When other translations are used, they will be underlined. Before a person takes on a leadership responsibility, they should count up the cost – carefully. Notice what *James 3:1* says: *"My brethren, be not many masters, knowing that we shall receive the greater condemnation."*

A leader will be held accountable in a stricter manner than his followers. James goes on to say: *"For in many things we offend all."* If that's an adequate reason for not stepping up to take the lead, no one will ever do so. Take a look at Moses; he was on the backside of the desert, keeping his father-in-law's sheep; when God called him to a leadership position. Moses was an educated man that had been accustomed to comforts and pleasures of the palace; was working in one of the lowest pursuits of his day, herding sheep.

Exodus 3:2; *"And the angel of the Lord appeared unto him in a flame of fire out of the midst of a bush: and he looked, and, behold, the bush burned with fire, and bush was not consumed."*

God does not necessarily call leaders because of their secular education or ability, nor their present position. Whom God calls, he will qualify them.

Notice *Psalms 32:8*; *"I will instruct thee and teach thee in the way which thou shalt go; I will guide thee with mine eye."*

And another promise is found in *Psalms 48:14*; *"For this God is our God for ever and ever: he will be our guide even unto death."*

Those God calls to leadership position, will have the assurance that they can rely on God's willingness and ability, to show them what His will is for them in that leadership role. God's method of accomplishing His plan and purpose is people. However, Moses didn't feel qualified for the task that God had given him; and he cried out to God with his question, "Who *am I?" (v. 11)*.

This question was so irrelevant that God did not even bother to answer it. God said, "Moses, it really does not matter who you are, certainly, I will be with you." What God is trying to point out to Moses was, "Whether you feel up to the task or not, the point is that I am going to be there." The statement "I made you," still holds – I am going to do it; and I am going to give you the privilege of being in it with me. You will be my instrument of deliverance."

THOSE WHOM GOD CALLS, HE QUALIFIES

Example #1
The call of Gideon: ***Judges 6:2;*** *"And the hand of Midian prevailed against Israel: and because of the midianites the children of Israel made them the dens which are in the mountains and caves, and strongholds."*

With a handful of men, he turned to fight the armies of the aliens. Was he always like that? Bold, courageous and waxing valiant in a fight? When God called Gideon, his first response was quite familiar to God.

Judges 6:15; *"And he said unto him, "Oh my Lord, wherewith shall I save Israel? Behold, my family is poor in Manasseh, and I am the least in my father's house."*

God said to Gideon, *"Surely I will be with thee, and thou shalt smite the Midianites as one man."* God said to him in effect, what he said to Moses. It doesn't matter that your family is poor, or that you are least in your father's house. The point is not who you are, but that *I will be with you.*

It's not a person's weakness that disqualifies them from being spiritual leaders, but it's God's strength; he will work through us. So if God calls you to a task and you have an overpowering sense of weakness, need, and inadequacy – rejoice! You are in good company. Men of God, down through the centuries, have felt the same way; but they also believed God to be sufficient for the task to which he had called them. "Be the leader you were meant to be" (v.13).

Example #2
Other calls then and now: Do you recall the last order of Jesus Christ to his followers? "Go and make disciples of all nations." Accompanying that command to them was the promise: "I will be with you always," in reference to ***Matt. 28:19,20 NIV.*** God is still saying to all of us today, "I am with you".

Paul described himself as "not meant to be called an apostle, because I persecuted the church of God" – ***1 Cor. 15:9.*** He also wrote, *"I thank Jesus Christ our Lord, who hath enabled me, for that he counted me faithful, putting me into the ministry; who was before a blasphemer, and a persecutor, and injurious"* – ***1 Timothy 1:12,13a.*** If ever a man had a background that will render him unqualified to be a Christian leader for God, it was the Apostle Paul. Yet he became a great leader to the Gentiles; and was used of God to write most of the New Testament.

Other men with undisciplined characters, as well as, great men of God, such as John Mark (see Acts 15:36-38) and David a Shepherd who tended sheep. So when God calls you to a task, let neither a sense of inadequacy or a "poor background" hinder you from following his lead. For God worketh in you, to will and to do by his good will.

Who is qualified to lead? "God," but he will choose ordinary men from every walk of life and qualify them to work with his plan and purpose; and exalt them to great positions in this life to be his leaders for this day and time.

"He that thinketh he is leading and has no one is following, is just taking a walk," Dr. John Maxwell, In Joy Life Leadership Seminar, 1990 Anaheim, Ca.

CHAPTER 15

How to Spot a Leader

Oftentimes, in our congregation and in the secular world, pastors, business owners, and presidents of corporations are looking for leaders. Pastors are looking for them to enhance their ministries and the secular world needs them to enhance their businesses. Dr. John Maxwell, in his 1990 "In Joy Life" seminar, gave four general observations on "How to Spot a Leader".

1. It takes one to know one.
2. It takes one to enlist one.
3. It takes one to keep one.
4. It takes one to produce one.

How to Spot a Leader

You should look for a person(s) who have influence; for a leader is anyone that has these two characteristics: (1) They are a person that's going somewhere and (2) They have the ability to persuade others to go along with them.

Next, you should look for the level of their influence; and who influences them, (birds of a feather flock together). Also consider, whom are they following.

Another observation is self-discipline. Take note to see if that person is trying to conquer the world or themselves. If they are trying to conquer the world, they lack discipline in their own lives. If they have themselves under strict discipline, it's a good quality of leadership. A good leader is emotionally stable. They will not allow the actions of the other to dictate reactions.

Time is important to leaders. It is important to know that there are two pains, in which we cannot escape and often we exchange. The first pain is discipline; the other is the pain of regret. The pain of discipline comes first; the pain of regret follows after. Here is the best reason for trading the pain of regret for the pain of discipline. "Discipline weighs ounces, and regret weighs tons," E. James Robin.

"There's only one thing more painful than learning from experience, and that is not learning from experience," stated Archibald McLeigh. According to Dr. John Maxwell, the following questions should be asked when checking a leader's track record:

1. What are your experiences?
2. What are your accomplishments?
3. Have your accomplishments included others, or just yourself?
4. Does your experience relate to what I need?
5. Can you do it again?
6. Can you do it better?
7. Will you do it again?

Strange People Skills

"You can get much farther with a kind word and a gun, than you can with a word alone," said Al Capone. Poor people skills will prohibit a person from building a reservoir of good will.

Years ago, Henry Ford asked a new car dealer to, switch the sign over his front entrance from, "Sales and Service" to "Service and Sales." Look for a person that has good problem-solving skills, for they have the ability to look beyond the object:

A. **_They are able to reject:_** They are always reviewing and looking for answers.
B. **_They have the ability to inquire:_** They are always asking questions and are aware of what is happening.
C. **_They are creative:_** They are always looking for a better way to do it.

Proverbs 16:9; "A man's heart deviseth his way: but the Lord directed his steps."
Proverbs 15:22; "With counsel purposes are disappointed: but in the multitude of counselors they are established."

1. **_Look for a person that just does not look for the "status quo."_**
   Latin for the "mess we are in". *"There is no future in any job; the future lies in the person who holds the job,"* Dr. George W. Crane.

2. **_Look for a person who is willing to take a risk._**
   "The reason mature people quit growing is that they are unwilling to risk failure," John Gardner.

3. **_Look for people that are willing to be different._**
   Many people are more comfortable with old problems, than with new positions. Peter Drucker says, *"The most common cause for executive failure is the inability or unwillingness to change with the demands of a new position. The executive, who keeps on doing what he has done successfully, is almost bound for failure."*

4. **_Look for people that are willing to pay the price._**
   There are no victories at bargain prices. Proponents or opponents decide the great issues, never by neutralists. The neutralists lose by default. *"Better it is to support one side or*

the other, than to do nothing and let another decide the issue for you; perhaps in a way you disapprove," Dwight Eisenhower.

5. *<u>Look for someone who can see the big picture.</u>*
   A. A leader has the foresight that others may not have.
   B. A leader has to stand when no one stands with him.
   C. A leader sees current as well as future needs.
   D. A leader is one whom is able to visualize moving the goal.

6. *<u>Look for someone who has the ability to handle stress.</u>*
   According to the National Association for Mental Health, here are eight ways to tell if the gauge is moving up inside you. Pastors and business owners need to observe potential leaders, and look for some of the following problems in their behaviors:

   A. Do minor problems and disappointments get under their skin and rule them more than they should?
   B. Do they find it hard to get along with people, and are people having trouble getting along with them?
   C. Investigate their social behavior to see if they still enjoy the things they used to enjoy; such as fishing, ball games, seeing a movie, etc.
   D. Investigate to see if their past still haunts them.
   E. Examine them to see if they are afraid of people and situations that never used to bother them.
   F. Observe them, to see if they are becoming suspicious of people that are around them, even their own friends.
   G. Observe their behaviors to see if they feel that they are trapped in their positions.
   H. Observe them to see if they feel inadequate, just not good enough to "hack it."

7. *<u>Look for someone who displays a positive attitude.</u>*
   "Look for the good and praise it" by William Arthur Ward. In everything, the good is there; our goal is to find it. In every person, the best is there; our job is to recognize it. In every situation, the positive is there; our responsibility is to provide it. In every problem, the answer is there; our responsibility is to provide it. In every setback, the victory is there; our adventure is to discover it. In every crisis, the reason is there, our challenge is to endure it. Be different, be original, be unique – look for the good and praise it.

Leadership is influence, and every positive influencer is a good leader, whether good or bad, God knows. **(Man look on the outward appearance, but God looks at the heart * 1 Samuel 16:7).**

NOTES

CHAPTER 16

The Cost of Effective Leadership

We can see the cost of effective leadership through illustrated story of Jesus going through Gergesenes.

Before Jesus came, there was a real problem in the country that no one could pass by that way. Yes, the people wanted someone to solve that problem, but they didn't want to lose their pigs. This reminded me of most church leaders: they want God to solve their problems without any cost. They want all the solutions, (my church board at that time) but they wanted them for nothing.

Even though Jesus solved the problem, the people were unsatisfied with the cost. Most leaders want deliverance without disturbance. They want benefits without the bills; success without sacrifice; but it just doesn't work that way.

Leadership includes discomfort:

If you are going to be an effective leader, you are going to experience a great amount of discomfort. We live in a culture that worships comfort: fast food restaurants, microwave ovens, instant potatoes, pre-cooked vegetables, automatic tellers, etc. We have learned how to control our environment with central heating and air conditioning; we have learned how to control pain, depression, and stress through medications. We want to play, but we don't want to pay the price; we want the position and the paycheck, but we don't want to do the work. Paul understood the cost he paid for his apostleship:

2 Cor. 11:23; *"Are they ministers of Christ? (I speak as a fool) I am more; in labours more abundant, in stripes above measure, in prisons more frequent, in deaths oft."*

24; *"Of the Jews five times received I forty stripes save one."*

25; *"Thrice was I beaten with rods, once was I stoned, thrice I suffered shipwreck, a night and a day I have been in the deep."*

26; *"In journeying often, in perils of waters, in perils of robbers, in perils by mine own countrymen, in perils by the heathen, in perils in the city, in perils in the wilderness, in perils in the sea, in perils among false brethren."*

27; *"In weariness and painfulness, in watchings often, in hunger and thirst, in fastings often, in cold and nakedness."*

28; *"Beside those things that are without, that which cometh upon me daily, the care of all the churches."*

29; *"Who is weak, and I am not weak? Who is offended, and I burn not?"*

Let us focus on three things that were uncomfortable to Paul's leadership from the above scriptures.

Leadership includes dissatisfaction:
Most men and women in the Bible who attained great leadership ability, all have been dissatisfied about something. Even though dissatisfied they sought God on how to accomplish the task. For example, Nehemiah rebuilt the walls around Jerusalem. Esther had to seek God about the destiny of her people. Moses could have stayed in Pharaoh's courts, enjoying all the pleasure and riches of Egypt, but he chooses to lead God's people out.

Leadership includes disruption:
If you are going to be an effective leader, you must get used to disruptions. Working with people does not guarantee smooth sailing. The moment we think we have it made, another hurting, needy person or problem comes along. Leaders will have to deal with disruptions; the issue is whether to respond or react to the disruption. To react means to act negatively. To respond means to act positively.

Leadership includes meeting needs:
    A. Effective leaders do not allow disruptions to throw them; they learn how to handle their disruptions. They don't allow disruptions to consume them.
    B. Effective leaders keep their eyes on their goals.
    C. A good leader will meet the need of others. As he or she presses on toward their own goals.

The following are three guidelines that will help you with disruptions:

1. *<u>Find out the specific will of God for your life.</u>*
   Nothing will keep you on track better than knowing God's purpose in your life. "Purpose is God's original intent," says Myles Monroe in "The Pursuit of Purpose."
2. *<u>Don't give in to the desires of the flesh.</u>*
   Effective leaders, who have paid the price, know the value of character building exercise. They know that they can't give into the fleshly desires; whether they are their own desires or other peoples.
3. *<u>Don't try to survive.</u>*
   Galatians 1:15; *"But when it pleased God, who separated me from my mother's womb, and called me by his grace."*
   16; *"To reveal his Son in me, that I might preach him among the heathen; immediately I conferred not with flesh and blood."*
   17; *"Neither went I up to Jerusalem to them which were apostles before me; but I went into Arabia, and returned again unto Damascus."*

Paul is telling us to never get comfortable.

Look at all the afflictions he went through; he was beaten, shipwrecked, abandoned, left for dead, in the sea a day and a half, put in prison, etc. What Paul is saying is "If comfort is our aim, we will miss out of the riches of the kingdom of God."

<u>Never allow for Plan "B"</u>

I am not talking about natural problems, but what I am talking about is; there is not a "Plan B" in the area of commitment to God's plan for you. Either you are committed or you are not. If you are going to be an effective leader, then you must get rid of the exit signs in your life. <u>Paul knew that he would just survive.</u>

Romans 8:35; *"Who shall separate us from the love of Christ? shall tribulation, or distress, or persecution, or famine, or nakedness, or peril, or sword?"*

36; *"As it is written, For thy sake we are killed all the day long; we are accounted as sheep for the slaughter."*

37; *"Nay, in all these things we are more than conquerors through him that loved us."*

38; *"For I am persuaded, that neither death, nor life, nor angels, nor principalities, nor powers, nor things present, nor things to come."*

Never fall into a maintaining mind-set.

An effective leader will never settle for the good, when the best is a possibility. A good leader is not satisfied, just maintaining the "status quo." An effective leader is willing and ready to make waves and suffer discomfort, to accomplish what God has called him to do. That's why being beaten, shipwrecked, abandoned, imprisoned and discomforted, didn't stop Paul from finishing his course. He fought a good fight, finished his work, and received his crown.

Once he knew what God wanted him to do, he didn't go to Jerusalem to ask the church; he simply headed in the direction God had told him to go. His goal wasn't just to survive; his goal was to please God.

If we are going to be effective leaders for God, we must understand that there is a cost each of us will have to pay, to accomplish what God has assigned us to do. We must (1) count up the cost; (2) be willing to pay the price; and (3) move forward, in spite of your discomfort, dissatisfaction, and disruptions. As effective leaders, our goals and properties should be to please God, not us or our friends. Remember, everybody will not give you praise for your God-given leadership abilities. There are still people that want you to solve their problems, but do not want to lose their pigs.

There is a cost for effective leadership and all leaders will have to count up the cost, either now or later. If you are going to be an effective leader, you will pay the cost!

NOTES

CHAPTER 17

Biblical Principles That Will Help Leaders Reach Their Potential

In this lesson, there will be some biblical principles that will help you reach your potential if they are followed. *Philippians 4:13;* "*I can do all things through Christ which strengthened me.*" Successful and unsuccessful people do not vary much in their capabilities. They vary in their desire to reach their potential. The first question you should ask yourself is, "What is my potential?" The only way you can please God is by knowing your potential.

Colossians 3:17; "*And whatsoever ye do in word or deed, do all in the name of the Lord Jesus, giving thanks to God and the Father by him.*"

1 Thessalonians 4:1; "*Furthermore then we beseech you, brethren, and exhort you by the Lord Jesus, that as ye have received of us how ye ought to walk and to please God, so ye would abound more and more.*"

1 Corinthians 9:24; "*Know ye not that they which run in a race run all, but one receiveth the prize? So run, that ye may obtain.*"

We are disloyal to God when we make small what He intends to make large through us. We need to understand the biblical description of contentment:

Two Ideas
1. I should have my desires limited to what I already have and that which I have already achieved laziness.
2. I should have my desires channeled to that which God wants me to have and what God wants me to achieve – leadership.

Biblical principles will help you reach your potential. *"Man's mind, once stretched by a new idea, never regains its original dimensions,"* Oliver Wendell Holmes.

Seven Steps to Stagnation:
1. We have never done it that way before.
2. We have tried that once before.
3. It won't work.
4. That's not my responsibility.
5. It can't be done.
6. It's not my fault.
7. We might fail.

Three Zones People Live In

- **Challenge Zone:**
  "I try to do what I haven't done. If you reach your potential you have advanced for future work."

- **Comfort Zone:**
  "I do what I know I can do. I am accomplishing my task for today."

- **Coasting Zone:**
  "I do not do what I have done – I rely on my past. That means I have not made my plans for my future. I must rely on my past, that's history; and if I continue to operate in the past, I am headed for certain failure."

An expert is a man who will know tomorrow, while the things he predicted yesterday didn't happen today. The British Parliament ordered a study of Thomas Edison's electric light bulb in 1878. The report concluded: Edison's ideas are good enough for our transatlantic friends, but unworthy of the attention of practical scientific men. You and I know the outcome of Edison's invention.

Expect great things to happen:
Our main limitation is our expectation. Remember we see what we are prepared to see – now that equals our attitudes. Secondly, what we see is what we get – now that equals accomplishment.

Devote yourself to something you do well:
People who reach their potential, spend more time asking, "What am I doing well?" rather than "What am I doing wrong?"

Don't take short cuts:
Zechariah 4:10; *"For who hath despised the day of small things? For they shall rejoice, and shall see the plummet in the hand of Zerubbabel with those seven; they are the eyes of the* Lord, *which run to and fro through the whole earth."*

If you take short cuts, you will not reach maturity in the following areas:

- Experience: There are some things in life you need to know, and if you bypass experience, you will suffer in the future.
- Discipline: Will keep you focused on your goals.

Jeremiah 48:10; "*Cursed be he that doeth the work of the Lord deceitfully, and cursed be he that keepeth back his sword from blood.*"

Lack of exposure:
If you lack exposure, you don't want to see the big picture, you will only see things through your eyes, and you should rely on the opinions of those who have seen the big picture.

Reliance on God:
Proverbs 3:6 – "*In all thy ways acknowledge him, and he shall direct thy paths.*"

Embrace discipline as a friend:
"*A man without decision of character can never be said to belong to himself. He belongs to whatever can make captive of him,*" John Foster.

Face your fears and fix them:
Henry Ford said, "*One of the great discoveries a man makes, is to find he can do what he was afraid he could not do.*" Most of the barriers we are bent against are in ourselves – we put them there- and we can take them down. *Proverbs 24:16* – "*For a just man falleth seven times, and riseth up again: but the wicked shall fall into mischief.*" "*People are never more insecure than when they became obsessed with fears at the expense of their dreams,*" by Norman Cousins.

Choose your close friends wisely:
Principle: "A person almost never rises above the level of his or her closest friendship." The most important lesson I've learned in leadership is those who are closest to me will determine my level of success.

Bring the best out of people you work with – "Power given, is power gained."
Rick Warren in his "Encouraging the Word Ministry" seminar says, "*You bring the best out of people by believing in them, encouraging them, sharing with them, trusting them.*"

Draw inspiration from God and other people:
Proverbs 13:20; "*He that walketh with wise men shall be wise: but a companion of fools shall be destroyed.*"

Have a mission that motivates you:
We will go where our dreams takes us.

Have a sense of social responsibility:
Giving something of value to others adds value and meaning to our own life. *"The greatest thing this generation can do is lay a few stepping stones for the next generation,"* said Charles F. Keating.

Do more than anticipate change – keep up with it and embrace it:
Harvard business professor, Ted Levitt says, *"The future belongs to the people who see possibilities, before they become obvious. You must change with the times, unless you are big enough to change the times."*

Dedicate your life to God:
D. L. Moody, founder of Moody Bible Institute says, *"If God is your partner, make your plans big."* John Wesley stated, *"Give me one hundred preachers who fear nothing but God, and I care not a straw, whether they are clergymen or laymen; such a love will shake the gates of hell and set up the kingdom of heaven on earth."*

If you apply these sixteen principles to your life daily, you will reach your God-given potential and will accomplish others goals as well.

NOTES

CHAPTER 18

Biblical Examples of Men Who Became Great Leaders through Good Mentoring

Does the Bible support the concept of mentoring? What references to mentors and mentees can we find in scripture? What principles, if any, can we learn from these references?

Although the Bible doesn't use the words mentor, mentee, or mentoring, it frequently refers to what we believe are successful mentoring relationships: Jesus and His disciples, Barnabas and Paul, Paul and Timothy, Naomi and Ruth, Elijah and Elisha, Moses and Joshua, Deborah and Barak, Elizabeth and Mary (the mother of Jesus), and many others. All are powerful examples of pairs and the *God-inspired actions* they took to help each other develop.

Moses and Joshua (Mentor and Mentee) aptly illustrate a successful mentoring partnership. Moses demonstrated the wisdom of a mentor by deciding to delegate an important task (Exodus 17:9). He placed one of his soldiers, Joshua, in command of a battle with the Amalekites over a water dispute. In making this decision, Moses demonstrated trust in Joshua's gifts and leadership potential. He opened the way for their ongoing teamwork. This is the first time this "mentor" asked someone else to lead an attack, one of many that his "mentee" Joshua would command.

Did they sit down and negotiate this developmental relationship, calling each other mentor and mentee? Probably not. It's more likely that Moses wasn't cognizant of applying mentoring principles and didn't necessarily regard Joshua as his mentee. Yet the ingredients of mentoring were there, and Joshua entered a relationship with a respected man that changed Joshua's life forever.

Following this successful assignment, Joshua became a frequent companion of Moses. Even though he was called a servant (e.g., Exodus 24:13, 33:11), he was actually more of a colleague. *(Notice Exodus 3:11. Joshua refused to leave with Moses, something that would not have been permitted of a servant.)* Their mentoring relationship deepened and Joshua gained valuable knowledge, skills, and confidence.

We find evidence that their mutual trust increased when Moses allowed his mentee to accompany him to an important meeting . . . with none other than God! (Exodus 24:13-14).

We're not sure that Joshua was actually with Moses in the presence of the Lord, but we know for certain that he was on the mountain (Exodus 32:17) and talked with Moses on their return to the camp. Imagine the incredible lessons Joshua received that day!

Moses took Joshua to another meeting in a special tent where Moses spoke with God again. Joshua chose to stay at the tent after Moses left to return to camp (Exodus 33:11). Joshua remained on his own in the presence of God. Moses demonstrated significant trust by not interfering in this major opportunity for Joshua.

Moses continued to offer Joshua opportunities to develop. He assigned him (along with 11 other men) to spy out the Promised Land. The mentor gave him a job that required a plan, teamwork, and a report (Numbers 13:16). Moses probably also provided some suggestions for how to carry out this plan.

Finally, Moses affirmed his mentee by commissioning Joshua in the presence of the people of Israel (Deuteronomy 31:7-8). He gave Joshua public recognition for the lessons he learned. What's more, Moses conferred power on his mentee, and vacated his position to him. Their formal mentoring relationship ended. When Moses died, Joshua was appointed as the new leader of Israel and later took his people into the Promised Land (Numbers 27:15-23).

Moses provided a great lesson in how to transfer leadership. A time comes to either step aside to allow our successors to lead in our place or allow them to move on to a place of leadership elsewhere. Moses gave the proper direction, teaching, and recognition to prepare Joshua to fulfill his role in life.

The mentoring relationship of Moses and Joshua was very task-and-performance oriented. They provide clear-cut illustrations of several excellent mentor activities:

- *assigning* the mentee preliminary stretch tasks;
- depending on the mentee's initial performance, making *additional assignments* requiring more skills and responsibilities;
- inviting them to *key events*;
- allowing the mentee to *observe the mentor* in action;
- *affirming* the mentee for achievements; and
- *stepping aside* to let the mentee succeed.

Jesus' private time with His disciples — away from the crowds (the pulpit and public times) — was the critical mentoring foundation for all that he did publicly. Pastors, too, need to get out of the pulpit to do mentoring. They must network into the life and fabric of the ones they mentor.

The term "mentor" is linked with a wise and trusted counselor or teacher. It was used about Odysseus's trusted counselor, in ancient Greek Mythology, where Athena became the guardian and teacher of Telemachus. Most major businesses, our armed forces officer's training, plus Christian groups and churches now use "mentor" to represent a special relational process.

DEFINITIONS OF MENTORING

- "It is a dynamic relationship of trust in which one person enables another to maximize the grace of God in their life and service." — *John Mallison* [2]

- "Mentoring is a relationship through which one person empowers another by sharing God-given resources." — *Robert Clinton* [3]

- "An agreed-upon exchange between two persons, a more experienced person and a less experienced person, developing the less experienced to their maximum potential in Christ and empowering them with abilities to meet a need, achieve a goal, or to grow through a situation." — *Murray and Owen.* [4]

The Bible is full of excellent examples of mentoring relationships. It's amazing to see spiritually hungry Elisha run past the other prophets to get to Elijah's side (2 Kings 2:1 - 16), passionate about being mentored. Follow David's growth as his mentor-peer, Jonathan, introduces him to political leadership. Other kings were mentored by their religious teachers.

In the New Testament our supreme model, Jesus Christ, mentored the Twelve and the Three. One of the three, Peter, in turn had some type of mentoring relationship with Barnabas (Galatians 2:11-13). Barnabas then imitated the method that he'd benefited from, by mentoring Mark and Paul. Through Paul, God erected a chain of Spirit-filled, world-changing mentors and church planters.

Let's look at five important mentoring elements involved in building a spiritual leader from scratch. It will cost you some personal time. We shoot for biblical *"koinonia."* The Greek word *"koinonia,"* translated fellowship, means "to share or to partner, to invest in." Amazingly, in the heart of an apprentice your time, words, attitudes, and actions are etched on their memory. They will quote you for years! Little is much when God is in it.

We will use these ideas: ***Principles & Promises, Progress, Problems, Prayer, and Practical ministry.*** These five elements are present in most meeting times or weeks that you invest in an individual. But their order may vary. For instance, perhaps someone needs help with a problem, or is yearning to pray over a need. That would be the first (but perhaps not my only) priority for our time together. Other times the mentee has a Bible question, and one goes from there. Let's take a more in-depth look at these five mentoring elements and how they allow us "to share and invest in" others.

PRINCIPLES & PROMISES
(Colossians 2:2b, 3; Colossians 3:16; 2 Peter 1:4)
Ultimately the mentor and mentee must have a structured time together in God's Word. We need a base and a focal point of agreement. John communicates Jesus' coming in this way: *"The Word became flesh and dwelt among us"* (John 1:14). Jesus perfectly lived out the *Word*. He fully revealed God's will through His life and words. Answers to questions, solutions to problems, standards for living — these all flow from Scripture. The foundation of any growing mentoring relationship will involve sharing and living the Word of God.

Author-professor Dr. Howard Hendricks was asked; "What is the first thing you try to do with the new convert?" Howard answered, *"First thing I do, is to get a person into Bible study."* The Bible is a book of principles to live by, and promises to believe and claim. Through Scripture God's fingers will touch every part of our lives. The mentor needs to model what he wants the mentee to do and be. In the area of "Principles" we are to be pacesetters, leading the mentee into Bible study.

When you meet for mentoring, always want to know *where they are* in the Scriptures. Can they feed themselves? Are they memorizing the Word? Do they know how to hear from God every day as they read and study the Bible? One characteristic that separates a baby from a teenager is the ability to feed oneself.

PROGRESS
(Hebrews 3:13; Ecclesiastes 8:11)
People do what we inspect, rather than what we expect. All of us need to be accountable. There is no biblical "lone wolf" Christianity! The Old Testament tells the story of the *people* of God. Jesus' parables unveil the *kingdom;* the epistles went primarily to *communities* of faith. We have little guidance on how to live as a follower alone, because God never intended it." [7] We are to care enough to lovingly challenge the mentee and help them be faithful to their commitment to the spiritual disciplines. One must show more patience, however, with a new convert. And with each person, we suggest lovingly, using much patience and encouragement.

Some kind of discipline is at the root of all mentoring; that is, if the mentoring process has true disciple-building as it's goal. God commands us to *"Exhort one another daily, while it is called Today, lest any of you be hardened though the deceitfulness of sin."* (Hebrews 3:13). To lovingly confront and ask for faithfulness in biblically-based and agreed-upon assignments — that lifts a sagging relationship, without focus, to one of strong growth-potential. On the other hand, a "no check-up" relationship blunts people from conviction and spiritual reproduction.

PRINCIPLES and PROGRESS
Mentoring is a deliberate, encouraging relationship in which the mentor seeks to spiritually lift another person to their full potential in Christ. The foundational element of the mentoring relationship, as well as the weekly time together, involves life-changing principles and

promises from the Word. We want to help the mentee discover the Bible as holy, inspired, and practical. Strive for measurable progress, including mutual accountability and check-up. Without some sense of "apprenticeship" on the part of the one mentored, sustained growth is difficult. Although mentoring may begin with teaching or counseling hours, the best mentoring needs a consistent schedule of an hour or more weekly, focused on both the mentee's needs but also on goals, which the mentor has for them.

Helping with PROBLEMS
(Psalm 119:130; Psalm 17:4; Ecclesiastes 10:1)
Many mentoring relationships have begun by listening to a person in crisis. But do "problem people" ever become problem-solvers? Yes! When they have a wise, loving mentor who knows how to lead them to *"Christ, in whom are hid all the treasures of wisdom and knowledge."* (Colossians 2:3).

Mentoring needs to be done by choice, rather than chance. We have to make a commitment toward that person, and them to us. Therefore, early on we need to clarify our expectations, if the friendship began as simply a loose time of counseling, for instance. This will neutralize potential relationship problems. Agree on a meeting place, a time and its length. Discuss together some perimeters about topics, goals, and how often you will meet. Get some agreement to complete a specific study or ministry you do together.

Eventually we'll have to confront, or correct. We become mirrors that help the mentees understand their blind spots and the attitudes that hinder God's best in their life. While Satan can't read our minds, he does log our journey. We must be aware that this potentially effective relationship will be under attack.

Problems That Kill a Mentee's Potential
The world is always trying to squeeze us into its mold. Every commercial on TV has one of three heart-motivations that it's tapping into to sell its product: the sex motive, the security motive, or the success motive. Mentoring men involves walking through the minefields of girls, gold, and glory (1 John 2:15-17). For women also, these same categories might be defined: *control, collect, compete.*

As in the Old West, we seek to "head the Enemy off at the pass." We counter-attack sexual temptations, "the lust of the flesh," before they are a problem by teaching self-denial and taking up one's cross daily. Instead of finding security in money, "the lust of the eyes," we train men and women to give their life, time, and money to Jesus. To counter the success drive for personal glory, "the pride of life," we model and teach the servant-heart attitude. We are on earth to *"please Him* **(Jesus)** *who hath chosen us to be a soldier."* (2 Timothy 2:4).

True mentoring is not an act but a process. It simply takes time. Who is sufficient for this kind of warfare? Not me! We listen patiently as the mentees shares their heart, their hurts and their hesitancies. Then through prayer we seek the wisdom of the Holy Spirit. *"The entrance of*

thy Word giveth light; it giveth understanding to the simple" (Psalm 119:130). The Holy Spirit will teach us how to customize His Word to each person's needs.

PRAYER
(Matthew 18:19; Isaiah 65:24; John 14:13, 14)
Perhaps the most bonding experience we can have is praying aloud regularly with another person. Prayer is a mentoring necessity. We need to pray specifically, openly, freely, crying out to God in intercession and petitions. Set aside time for prayer together, whenever you meet to mentor. Be careful how you pray. You are modeling.

Expand the prayer horizon of your mentee. Pray driving in a car. Pray over the phone. Pray together as you walk down a street. In a restaurant you can pray with eyes open. Make a list of the mentee's prayer needs and pray daily. Ask the mentee about his problems in prayer and answers. Help him also make up a prayer list, and log the answers. Sometimes the pressure on the mentee is such that we need to read some passage of Scripture to claim, and go immediately into prayer. There are examples for us of prayers God loves to hear and answer. These other prayers of Paul are also worth memorizing:

Ephesians 1:17-20;
Philippians 1:9-11;
Colossians 1:9-12;
1 Thessalonians 5:12, 13;
2 Thessalonians 1:11, 12.

***PRACTICAL* Ministries**
(Ecclesiastes 9:10; Ephesians 6:6; Colossians 3:23, 24)
Next to prayer, ministry together is a great bonding experience. It also quickly reveals what principles you've taught the mentee that are sticking. Without ministry together, you'll never know what they truly knows! Take someone out witnessing, and you'll discover quickly where they are in practical knowledge. Their questions later will be pointed and real. No room for "theory" here! When the mentee begins to do ministry, their real fears, weaknesses, and gifts begin to surface. Then, your progress in helping them into Christlikeness will accelerate.

Remember, in ministry you're modeling <u>all</u> the time. A Pastor told this story: When pastoring, I recall taking Charlie with me to give a Gospel presentation to a young couple. The couple gave their hearts to Christ. Charlie was thrilled. Ten years later I visited with Charlie in another city where he was now director of a statewide medical work. "Remember the first time you took me witnessing? Remember that illustration you used?" Charlie asked, smiling. "No," I replied. Charlie went on to explain the illustration I'd used. "That couple came to Christ. And I've used that illustration every time I've given the Gospel the past 10 years!" "Oh, Charlie," I replied, "that's not even my <u>best</u> illustration!" Charlie's instant comment was, "I saw it work when they got saved; so it's what I use."

Mark it well: THE METHOD IS THE MESSAGE, too. Paul commanded the Philippians, ***"Those things which you have both learned and received, and heard and seen in me, do, and the God of peace shall be with you"*** (Philippians 4:9). Reverse the first phrase of the verse, and note the progression: seen, heard, received and learned. We learn by watching what a mentor does and says; we begin to digest it, and ultimately copy it.

Decide together where and when to meet for ministry. At first, it may be helping with a cookout at the church, mowing a widow's yard, painting a house, visiting a patient in the hospital, or helping a neighbor with a computer need. After a time of ministry, we then go out for coffee and discuss and evaluate the ministry. What did we do? What could we have done better? We're listening all the time for the mentee's response — their questions, comments, emotional state, and growth. Then in private we'll do follow-up prayer about the ministry that next week.

Let's review these five elements. As God makes us available to mentor, we link up in heart with a people through Bible principles. We help their progress in accountability and assignments. We bond through prayer, solve problems together, and get out of the "holy huddle" in practical ministry. However, nothing is "in concrete." Only the Holy Spirit can change a person. As we mentor others, continual crying out to God for a holy walk in the Spirit, to be ready for those that God is preparing. Then as we encourage and carefully model what God has taught us, the Spirit will deepen the mentee's love for Jesus.

In this process of mentoring, God blesses the mentor exceedingly. The longer you mentor, the "richer" you are in blessings. With a heart to mentor, you'll never lack ministry. Claim Isaiah 43:4, ***"Since thou wast precious in my sight, thou hast been honorable, and I have loved thee: therefore will I give men for thee, and people for thy life."***

NOTES

NOTES

CHAPTER 19

Decision: The Key of Leadership

According to Calvin Miller in his book "An Influencer Discussion Guide on Leadership" says, *"Decision – the key to leadership. Leaders, whatever their professions of harmony, do not shun conflict; they confront it, exploit it, and ultimately embody it."*

Calvin Miller focuses on 2 Samuel 1-15 and 7:1-13, to support his comments on "decision, the key to leadership." In this passage of scripture, we see that Israel has a proud new capital, Jerusalem, which means "city of peace," but David realized it would become a city of turmoil, if God did not direct the nation from its very center. Since the Ark of the Covenant symbolized God's presence on earth, it needs to be within the walls of Jerusalem.

Like all great leaders, David was decisive. For him, all decision-making began and ended with God. His need to move the Ark into Jerusalem was based on his convictions. Great leaders make decisions after they have consulted with God. So David's decision to bring the ark to Jerusalem, the pure decision was based on the smaller decision of his monarchy. Every leader must know how to make pure decisions. Pure decisions are those that take place with God at the center of things.

"It ain't nothing till I call it," All American Umpire. "Two roads diverged in a wood, and I took the one less traveled by; and that made all the difference."

Calvin Miller goes on to say pure decisions serve in four ways:

1. They divide life into manageable segments.
2. They create new beginnings.
3. They contribute to a strong sense of self.
4. They focus us into lifelong participation with God that leads to meaningful living.

   I. Let us examine how decisions divide life into manageable segments.
   David never forgot the day he brought the Ark of the Covenant into the Holy City. It became for him, the milestone of his long, productive reign.

II. *They create new beginnings.*

Right or wrong decisions, create places for us to start again. A fresh start is always welcome. A good, firm decision can provide a place at which to choose a new direction. Certainly, David must have had criticism of his administration, perhaps his decision to bring the Ark into the Holy City. He acted in the face of criticism, and became a stronger person, after having made the decision. When leaders exercise personal courage, they will always become stronger.

III. *Decisions always serve our sense of self-worth.*

A sense of self-worth reminds us of our responsibilities for our own life and fortune. Decisive lifestyles teach, that to a large part, we manage our own selves, piece by piece, as a carpenter builds a house, we do indeed, make ourselves.

IV. *Decisions create a sense of self by forcing us into the cauldrons of refining loneliness.*

Others may help you clarify decisions; but we must decide alone. Decision-making makes you a partner with God. The insecurity of decision-making clearly shows that in order to do right, it is necessary to be on God's side. All of us should be aware that fifty percent of all the decisions we make will be wrong; but God can make a difference in lowering that percentage.

Dr. John Maxwell, author of "Your Attitude-Key to Success" wrote, ***"Great decisions are often as much a matter of timing as the event."***

1. The wrong decision at the wrong time = disaster.
2. The wrong decision at the right time = mistake.
3. The right decision at the wrong time = unacceptable.
4. The right decision at the right time = success.

If leaders would examine the life of David, they would find principles of decision-making. Christian leaders should learn from the biblical examples David left on record for us. All Christian leaders should seek God for understanding, of how to make the right choices.

Proverbs 3:6; *"In all thy ways acknowledge him, and he shall direct thy paths."*

Jeremiah 10:22; *"Behold, the noise of the bruit is come, and a great commotion out of the north country, to make the cities of Judah desolate, and a den of dragons."*

Philippians 4:6; *"Be careful for nothing; but in everything by prayer and supplication with thanksgiving let your request be made known unto God."*

Good decision-making wants God near at hand. The tabernacle was really a portable cathedral, made of rich hangings, costly gold, and brazen fixtures. The tabernacle and the Ark had been built by divine order during Israel's wilderness sojourn; that lasted for forty years. When David came to kingship; the Ark, at last, came to dwell within the security of a walled fortress (2 Samuel 6:2). David was a leader that had learned to seek God before he made any decisions.

> ***Psalms 51:10;*** *"Create in me a clean heart, O God; and renew a right spirit within me."*
>
> ***11;*** *"Cast me not away from thy presence; and take not thy holy spirit from me."*
>
> ***12;*** *"Restore unto me the joy of thy salvation; and uphold me with thy free spirit."*

The scripture indicated that leaders are sometimes forced to make decisions, on occasions when they feel God is far away. Oftentimes in our life, we have found ourselves saying, "God where are you? I need you now." I have learned in the times I thought he was far away, that's when he was the closest.

> ***Hebrews 13:5;*** *"Let your conversation be without covetousness; and be content with such things as ye have: for he hath said, I will never leave thee, nor forsake thee."*
>
> ***James 4:8;*** *"Draw nigh to God, and he will draw nigh to you. Cleanse your hands, ye sinners; and purify your hearts, ye double minded."*

When we draw near to God, He will always draw near to us. How do we draw near to God? In prayer and studying God's word daily. Leaders can't be double-minded. In decision-making, you must be single-minded. That's why, in all our ways, we must acknowledge God, and He will direct our paths.

"*Two roads diverged in a woods; and I took the one less traveled by, and that has made all the difference,*" by Robert Frost.

Decisions- right or wrong – will determine the success of your leadership.

NOTES

CHAPTER 20

How Leaders Perceive Themselves

As biblical leaders, we should have a healthy self-image, and the best way to create a good healthy self-image is to be honest about self-definition. "I would like to sing, but I can't." "No more Mr. Nice Guy."

If we do not evaluate our own behavior, or if we do not act to improve our conduct, it is below our standards, we will not fulfill our needs to be worthwhile, and we will suffer as acutely as when we fail to love or be loved.

"Morals, standards, values, or right and wrong behaviors are all intimately related to the fulfillment of our needs for self-worth," William Glassier.

As leaders, you will do God no real favors if you charge out into the world with no real understanding – of who you are. Did David understand who he was? Let's see how much he really knew about who he was and what God expected of him (Samuel 17:19-54). Before David could conquer the outward giant (Goliath) he had to conquer the inner enemy. Leaders fail to develop into what God has purposed for them. The chief reason they fail to conquer the enemy on the inside. Also, they fail to learn to subdue the flesh.

> Abraham Maslow, in his book called, "Toward a Psychology of Being," concludes that persons with low self-esteem and are not more frenzied in their lifestyles, are also less imaginative. They are therefore, far less likely to become a successful leader than a person who has better learned to manage the tough inner fear of self.

David's competence didn't come from a grumbled, powerful latent egoism. His dependence was upon God. Christian leaders sometimes make the mistake of pretending that their faith in God means an automatic self-esteem. Good self-esteem is imperative in the life of every leader. But what is self-esteem? Stanley Cooper defines self-esteem as, *"the evaluation, which the individual makes as customarily maintains with regard to himself."* It expresses an attitude of approval or disapproval and indicates the extent to which the individual believes himself to be capable, significant, successful, and worthy. In a Wall Street Journal article it reads, *"People of low self-esteem could manage, but never lead."* One thing for sure, the article goes on to say, *"That no one is really eager to be managed, while the entire world is hungry to lead."* Consider the powerful truth of these words: ***"If you want to manage somebody, manage yourself. Do that well and you will be ready to stop managing and start leading."*** This article was subtitled, "Let's Get Rid of Management." Often managers only manage what leaders have brought to being.

In this bible study, we should see that the only adequate mirror to high self-esteem is trusting God's knowledge and ability. Once David found out what God wanted with the direction of his leadership it was decided; it's not a difficult thing to lead once you see your leadership as part of God's overall plan for this world.

Seeing and accepting your God-given strength will make you useable to the God who gave them to you. Calvin Miller in his book, "An Influence Discussion Guide on Leadership," gives seven reasons how leaders perceive.

1. <u>The Leaders Hard Work of Self Analysis</u>

David knew what he had accomplished with God. Power made him a spiritual leader.

1 Samuel 17:26; *"And David spake to the men that stood by him, saying, What shall be done to the man that killeth this Philistine, and taketh away the reproach from Israel? for who is this uncircumcised Philistine, that he should defy the armies of the living God?"*

2. <u>Leaders Must Get God Involved In Self Study</u>

David was demoralized by Eliab's criticism that he was more a shepherd than a solider.

1 Samuel 17:28; *"And Eliab his eldest brother heard when he spake unto the men; and Eliab's anger was kindled against David, and he said, Why camest thou down hither? and with whom hast thou left those few sheep in the wilderness? I know thy pride, and the naughtiness of thine heart; for thou art come down that thou mightest see the battle."*

David had to develop stronger views of himself than his brother Eliab.

3. <u>Letting Your Past Guide Your Future</u>

1 Samuel 17:34; *"And David said unto Saul, Thy servant kept his father's sheep, and there came a lion, and a bear, and took a lamb out of the flock."*

35; *"And I went out after him, and smote him, and delivered it out of his mouth: and when he arose against me, I caught him by his beard, and smote him, and slew him."*

36; *"Thy servant slew both the lion and the bear: and this uncircumcised Philistine shall be as one of them, seeing he hath defied the armies of the living God."*

David had confidence in God because of past experiences. The confidence and assurance you have in God today will help direct your future performance for God.

4. *__Leadership and Traditional Thinking__*

1 Samuel 17:38; "And Saul armed David with his armour, and he put an helmet of brass upon his head; also he armed him with a coat of mail."

39; "And David girded his sword upon his armour, and he assayed to go; for he had not proved it. And David said unto Saul, I cannot go with these; for I have not proved them. And David put them off him."
    David was willing to succeed in traditional ways, yet he refused the customary battle attire.

5. *__Dealing with Criticism__*

1 Samuel 17:42; "And when the Philistine looked about, and saw David, he disdained him: for he was but a youth, and ruddy, and of a fair countenance."

43; "And the Philistine said unto David, Am I a dog, that thou comest to me with staves? And the Philistine cursed David by his gods."

    A.   Self-confidence survives under the attack of enemies.
    B.   A leader must know what sort of criticism debilitates him the most.

6. *__The Issue of Reputation__*

1 Samuel 17:46; "This day will the Lord deliver thee into mine hand; and I will smite thee, and take thine head from thee; and I will give the carcases of the host of the Philistines this day unto the fowls of the air, and to the wild beasts of the earth; that all the earth may know that there is a God in Israel."

47; "And all this assembly shall know that the Lord saveth not with sword and spear: for the battle is the Lord's, and he will give you into our hands."

    A.   David learned that a spiritual leader evaluates what his success will mean in terms of his reputation of God being magnified.
    B.   Great leaders are always aware of how their careers make God look in the eyes of others.

7. *__The Paralysis of Analysis__*

1 Samuel 17:53; "And the children of Israel returned from chasing after the Philistines, and they spoiled their tents."

54; "And David took the head of the Philistine, and brought it to Jerusalem; but he put his armour in his tent."

After a great deal of challenge and introspect, David incited the whole army of Israel to attack. Christians should never allow self-examination to become a substitute for real action. Godly leaders should never evaluate themselves by their own measurement. *"Any fool count the seeds in an apple, but only God can count the apple in a seed,"* Robert Schuller. *"Everything rises and falls on leadership,"* Dr. John Maxwell. Christians should see themselves as a vessel in God's hand doing the thing that God has created them to do.

Paul said, *"I can do all things through Christ that strengthens me,"* in Philippians 4:3. No human being can exist for long with shouting some sense of his own significance, whether he gets it by shooting random victims on the street, or by constructive work, or by rebellion, or by psychotic demands, in a hospital, or by Walter Mitty fantasies, he must be able to feel this, *"I count for something and be able to live that felt significance,"* Rollo May.

Finally, in our churches, homes, and jobs, when things are not operating and performance is dropping, remember there is never a "people problem," but a "lack of leadership" problem.

Isaiah 3:12; *"As for my people, children are their oppressors, and women rule over them. O my people, they which lead thee cause thee to err, and destroy the way of thy paths."*

If our churches are to continue to grow to meet the needs of this generation, then the church at large must start now implementing training programs for future leaders. The world seems to always catch the vision before the church. Currently, all of the major corporations are spending millions of dollars training men and women for advancement of their business for the future. The church must catch the vision, that God is the same, but the people are constantly changing. God needs Christian leaders to move his natural and spiritual church in this twenty-first century. Leaders are born daily, but effective leaders need to be equipped to meet the need of this confused generation. My purpose for writing this dissertation is to present church leaders with some biblical leadership principles that help pastors, elders, and church administrators with some godly principles, and examples of biblical men who've reached their potential through good mentors and some that pioneered the way for others. The attitudes of the church leaders elevate the attitudes of their followers. I hope in this study I have presented godly leaders if they are willing to apply these proven principles.

CHAPTER 21

"Clergy Self Care – Finding a Balance for Effective Ministry"

Each of us makes a powerful theological statement the moment we enter a room. People take one look at us and immediately determine something about our self-image, how we are managing our sexuality, the level of our self-care, our openness to learn and grow, our enthusiasm or lack of it, etc. How do they make such a judgment? Theorists claim that only fifteen (15) percent of what we communicate is verbal; the rest, eighty-five (85) percent, comes through nonverbally.

The fact that so much is communicated nonverbally should be sobering and challenging to us as clergy. Exactly what are we communicating through our body language, facial expressions, posture, skin tone, eyes, voice tone and texture, speed or slowness of speech, gestures, dress, intensity and affect, breathing rate, level of fatigue or vitality? Whether we like it or not, our health (or lack of it) is out there for the entire world to see.

It is very difficult for us to be agents of good news when we are either stressed out or burned out. We may say all the right things from the pulpit or leadership position, but communicate the opposite. A stressed-out pastor (clergyperson) may think they are responding to people in a loving way, but their nonverbal cues will give away the stress in their body every time. When a burned-out pastor makes a hospital call, he may say the right words and pray the right prayer, but still communicate that he would rather be somewhere else. It's a double message, and the nonverbal message usually predominates.

Approximately twenty (20) percent of clergy score extremely high on the Clergy Burnout Inventory. Among clergy in long pastorates (ten years or more) the number jumps to fifty (50) percent. The number is lower for younger clergy who generally score higher on stress scales than on the burnout inventory. The tragedy is that our best clergy, the hard working dedicated folk who have given too much of themselves for too long without replenishing the cup-are burning out. These burned-out clergy usually become dull, hollow, and uninteresting. When you meet them there is little to excite you. You don't want to get to know them better.

A pastor in this condition will not attract people in droves to his church. The Alban Institute Study on Assimilation of New Members discovered that newcomers wanted to "get a fix" on the clergy person very early on. They wanted to know whether or not the pastor was a "good enough" religious authority: Was he trust-worthy? Did he have a quality of being? Did he express a sense of caring that felt authentic? Newcomers "sized up" the pastor more by what he communicated nonverbally than by what was said. Even if newcomers were attracted to a parish for other reasons, they would not join unless they felt good about the pastor. *[Frankly speaking, visitors are also influenced in making decisions regarding joining churches by their interaction with other church leaders – non-credential holding lay-people, ministers, elders, evangelists, etc. and sometimes decline in joining due to negative experiences with them.]*

What are you communicating to your congregation right now? Are you displaying overwhelming tiredness or a sense of being grateful to be alive and to be in ministry with God's people? If your energy level is low, getting the words right won't make a difference. If you're upset or distraught, working harder and smiling stiffly won't fool anybody. <u>The only way we will be a healthy presence among our people is to keep ourselves healthy. That's where self-care comes in – doing all that is necessary to win out against the twin destroyers, stress and burnout.</u>

Narcissism vs. Self-Care

In seminars with pastors, tension in the room rises when the subject of self-care comes up. It just doesn't set right with some clergy. Some unconscious tapes play in their minds telling them that taking care of self is somehow unchristian or at least unnecessary. Early on in life the message was hammered home that the acceptable route in life involved sacrifice and hard work. In my family you could get your ears pulled if you got too hung up on yourself. Combine this early upbringing with a theology of commitment and sacrifice for the sake of the Gospel, and self-care got pushed down very low on the totem pole.

Given these unconscious processes, it's no wonder that clergy who do take care of themselves are sometimes viewed suspiciously. They're taking the soft path, rather than the path we've been taught, the one with all the thorns and rocks. Yet self-care, rightly understood, does not imply copping out and retiring to a lawn chair for the rest of our lives. We must hold on to the notion that the ordained ministry is special and costly. Ministry is not going to work if it refuses to engage with people who are struggling. Preaching at people from an antiseptic place of safety just won't cut it. At the same time, failing to be a good steward of our life and health won't do our ministries or our self any good either.

Another reason clergy seem to resist greater self-care is their fears about being identified with the "me" generation. Clergy born before the baby boom period seem to be particularly sensitive about this. It is true that a kind of narcissism plagues prosperous western cultures. Some would call it an epidemic. Many people are totally self-indulgent. After all, they say, isn't life, liberty, and the pursuit of our happiness our right? They become so absorbed with themselves that they fail to see life as a gift, relationships as Grace, and meaningful work as a privilege. They miss the point that the foundation of prayer is gratitude and instead demand of God what they regard as rightfully theirs.

Self-care can become destructive self-indulgence, but it can also be quite different from that. Again, we need to strike some kind of balance. We'll never get the balance exactly right, and when we do, it won't last long because some new stressor will tip the scale again. But working at that balance day by day pays off in the long run.

Self-care is little more than being a steward of some special gifts or a physical body with its enormous resilience and beauty, the capacity to nurture others and be nurtured in return, the capacity to enjoy immense sensual pleasure through such simple things as the splash of orange juice in our throats in the morning or a child in our lap.

I like to think of self-care as a commitment we make to God when we accept the role of resident religious authority. When we accept the call to be an agent of Grace, we simultaneously promise to forgo the easy life in self-indulgence, which can be a stumbling block to God's agents. I have come to call this "self-care for the sake of the kingdom". I take care of myself, not only for my sake, or in gratitude for the life given me by God, but also for the sake of others. If I don't take care of myself, I not only hurt myself, but I let others down as well.

At clergy workshops, participants are asked; "Would you feel some anger if you paid a handsome tuition to attend an Leadership seminar led by Bishop Charles Blake Sr., and the instructor showed up sixty pounds overweight, clothes reeking from smoke, and seemingly depressed and distracted?" Usually participants say "yes," they would feel cheated. Members of our congregations probably are similarly disappointed when they come to church and their pastor is too stressed to listen to them and too burned out to show any real caring.

What does good self-care look like? The term optimum health may provide some glimpses. This means striving for the best that we can be given our age, genes, liabilities and disabilities, and life experiences. Forget about trying to be like Denzel Washington or Halle Berry, what are the attitudes, disciplines, and lifestyles that bring out the best in us?

You may think, "I'm fifty-five, short, bald, walk with a limp, and have a hooked nose". Well, let's look at two clergy who fit that description. One remains trim and has, through therapy and a quality support group, gained appositive self-image. He has found ways to consistently deepen his spiritual side. Parishioners love his vitality and sense of humor. The older women in the congregation think of him as sexy and attractive.

The other pastor with similar statistics is overweight, depressed, cynical, and just trying to hang on until retirement. There is a myth in most denominations that pastors over age fifty don't receive calls to another church. The first pastor described, once he gets an initial interview, would receive a call. The second pastor probably wouldn't. The difference between the two is obvious and it has to do with how they take care of themselves.

Optimum health means managing our lives in such a way that we consistently maintain our physical, emotional, intellectual, and spiritual well-being. Helen Keller was the best she could be even though she was both blind and deaf. Someone in a wheelchair, paralyzed from the neck down, can be a constant delight because of her humor and spiritual depth. Whatever cards life has dealt us, our genes, our family of origin, our traumas and tragedies, and our friends, the spiritual task before us is to take that stack of cards and shuffle them in such a way that we come up positive, joyful, grateful, and humble. Then, we can offer ourselves to church and society.

Our chief task here on earth is to learn and grow. Unfortunately, in our culture we usually think of learning and growing strictly in terms of our intellects. So we have bright, capable people who are infantile in their emotional lives, shallow spiritually, and unable to manage the craving and addictions of their bodies. As they consistently sabotage themselves with their excesses we shake our heads: "He has so much to offer".

We need to learn to take care of ourselves in all areas of our lives, finding that balance between healthy self-care and unhealthy narcissism. Sometimes that process may get downright complicated. For example, there may be times when we are working through a difficult passage in our lives and our bodies simply need more sleep. Stress can be quite demanding on the body and psyche, and fatigue is to be expected. At such times it's important to give ourselves permission to sleep in. There are other times, however, when what our body really needs is a brisk walk before breakfast, not a few more minutes in a warm bed. We need to be able to discern what our bodies are really telling us.

If all of this sounds too difficult, it need not be. There will be aspects of wellness that are harder for us. Yet after the struggle, there comes the joy of feeling good. In fact, we may reach levels of joy we never thought possible. From this place of wellness, we can feel confident in inviting others to join us. It is out of this crucible that effective ministry comes.

What it Means to be in the Health and Wholeness Business

Amidst the many and sometimes seemingly impossible demands of pastoral ministry, we have opportunities to intervene in people's lives in ways unknown to other professionals. Sure, we have to earn our credibility with parishioners. It is not something conferred upon us just because we are pastors. Even so, we have unusual access to people. We can walk into people's offices or visit them in their homes and voice our concerns about what is happening in their lives. They may not agree with us but more than likely they will give us a hearing and perhaps even thank us for our concern. There is no other role in society that has that kind of access or authority.

Of course, parishioners expect clergy to guide them in their spiritual lives, but that is not the limit of our influence. We interact with people when they have physical, emotional, and intellectual concerns as well. When people are sick, we visit them in the hospital or at home and are expected to pray for them. When people have emotional problems, we make ourselves available for pastoral counseling. When people don't understand their life situation, we help them think things through intellectually so they can function better. (In fact, pastors soon learn that the doorway to a person's spiritual life is often through one of the other dimensions.) Clergy are still at the top of the list of those individuals they turn to when they have a problem.

The ministry is one of the only true generalist professions left in our society. While all other professions are becoming more and more specialized, we as clergy are still given authority to look at the whole picture, one's body stewardship, the quality of one's relationships, one's values, beliefs, and morals. Being a generalist may feel uncomfortable at times because we are not able to claim expertise in one slice of life. As a pastor, I longed to do something specific and concrete for people, like stitching up a wound of facilitation loan. At times I forgot that my specialty was being the one who cared about the total well-being of parishioners.

What it came down to is this: as generalist, we are in the health and wholeness business. To do well in our generalist role requires that we work diligently to nurture our own well being in each of the four dimensions. If I seriously want to be a better pastor, I first need to ask myself, "How can I be a healthier, more whole person? Staying healthy in each other of the four areas is hard unending work. It's like trying to herd a flock of sheep through a meadow. You run to one end to get some sheep in line, then back to the middle, then over to the other side. This year, I may need to go on a serious diet to embark on an exercise regimen to get my body in shape. Next, year, I may need therapy because my emotional well-being is in jeopardy. Later on, I may need to get my brain out of low gear and learn something new. One of the four areas will probably hold me back from achieving greater total health.

I find it helpful to visualize the components of health on the continuum from one to ten:

Physical Health

-1_____5_____+10

Emotional Health

-1_____5_____+10

Intellectual Health

-1_____5_____+10

Spiritual Health

-1_____5_____+10

When you are in the 'below five zone', you are functioning pathologically in that dimension. You may need a professional to help me get to five at least (being functional again). Then you will be able to do things for yourself to move higher. Anything you do to increase your health in one area automatically increases our health in the remaining three areas. Conversely, when your health diminishes in one area, it negatively affects your health on the minus side, 5 at the center, and 10 at the end of the plus side, we might rate ourselves as follows: Physical Health-6, Emotional Health-3, Spiritual Health-4, and Intellectual Health-8. This helps us focus our attention on what we have going for us in terms of total health and which areas in our lives need work and attention.

Viewing Health Holistically - A Counterculture Idea

In our culture, ninety-five (95) percent of medical professionals deal mainly with physical pathology. Some would say that doctors know a lot about illness, but on the medical model. When we have pain somewhere, our doctors tell us, 'Well let's do some test to see what's not working well.' With great efficiency, considering the complexity of certain medical problems, they are able to locate the difficulty. Then we take pills or have surgery. Most of the time we become functional again, but physicians usually don't help us reflect on what might be out of kilter in our lives that caused the illness in the first place.

Holistic health professionals do medical tests, too, but they also help us locate the dysfunctional parts of our lives that might have contributed to our illness. The health care would ask what we were eating, whether were exercising, what's happening at our job, whether we are having any fun, how things are going in our family. Because this kind of care takes about five times longer than a traditional doctor's visit, holistic physicians would make less money and we would probably not want to pay them the extra time either. Instead, we make mass appointments with our spiritual director, therapist, physician or surgeon, all of whom operate independently of one another. None of them ever gets the whole picture or our wellness or our illness. As a result, we learn very little about prevention. To move ourselves from the minus to the plus side of the continuum, we need to look elsewhere. Books, magazine articles, and friends have probably taught you more about such things as diet, exercise, the healing power of laughter, and nutrition than anything you learned from medical professionals.

Where the medical model consistently lets us down is helping us adopt a healthier life style before we get sick. A father never got any medical attention until after he had a major heart attack at the age of fifty-six. The truth is, his arteries had been corroding for ten years; he was overweight, smoked, eat the same kind of food he grew up on as a farm boy, meat, eggs, butter, fatty deserts and he exercised sporadically. Yet the first time anyone talked to him about his lifestyle was after he had a heart attack. The medical profession is doing more in the area of prevention theses days, but not enough. We need to take responsibility for our overall health and not leave it to others.

Staying healthy emotionally is an equally tough challenge for a pastor. It is difficult to keep any kind of emotional equilibrium as we move with our congregations through birth, deaths, marriages, divorces, and difficulties with children, retirement, etc. In addition, it is difficult to maintain a quality family life when we routinely work sixty to eighty hours each week. And time pressure often precludes clergy being a part of a support group that could nurture a healthier emotional life.

Staying healthy intellectually is a challenge for some clergy, too. Many let their minds go to sleep and haven't cracked a stimulating book in years. According to Mark Rough in his book Competent Ministry, only twenty (20) percent of clergy in the U.S. engage in regular continuing education events of five days or more each year. Matthew Fox claims that clergy's worst sin against the church is not being heretical or unethical, but being just plain dull. Have we lost the ability to fire the imaginations of the brightest and the best in this country?

Even though religion is our business, staying healthy spiritually remains a significant challenge for the clergy. We're supposed to be experts on spiritual matters, but we get little support for taking regular time to feed our spiritual hunger. Throughout seminary, we are fed a steady diet of daily chapel attendance, but are given next to no advice on how to feed ourselves spiritually when we leave the seminary community *(fortunately, this is less of a historic problem for the Black American Pentecostal church community, which is grounded in bible study, prayer and fasting. Yet, the discipline of developing and maintaining spiritual strength belongs to the oldest components of the Christian tradition)*.

As you might have guessed, I'm unimpressed with the quality of help we get to stay healthy in the physical, emotional, or spiritual realms. Yet it remains true that the quality of our ministry depends on our consistently pursuing greater health in each of those arenas of life.

Toward Theology of Self-Care

There was a presentation at a pastor's seminars on the need for physical exercise to keep the cardiovascular system healthy. Pastor Joe came up and said, 'There is nothing more boring than exercise.' He was a big man, easily fifty pounds overweight. 'Is there anything you like doing', he was asked. 'I like to golf', he responded. 'How often do you play?' he replied. "Once a week in warm weather, if I'm lucky. Usually there is something that happens at the local church that pre-empts my game." As we talked, I discovered that Joe spent sixty to seventy hours a week in the church. I wondered if a little scare tactic might reach him. 'Are you aware that you are killing yourself with your lifestyle?' I asked. He responded, "If God wants to take me, I'm ready. Who needs this vale of tears anyway?' His anger and depression were apparent.

Joe is not like many clergies. Not only are they not taking care of themselves, but they often use a sort of eschatological fatalism to justify their lack of self-care. They feel that they expend themselves completely in the Lord's work; God will look after them, body, mind and spirit. Their future is secure. Because the final goal is to be with the Lord, it is all right to mortgage one's body against this final eventuality.

As I've looked at my own life and talked to pastors, it's clear to me that much of what we do in ministry is governed by our theology of ministry. I began my ministry with the idea that I could singlehandedly make the small mission congregation to which I had been called grow and flourish. Seminary had prepared me intellectually for theological and biblical work with parishioners, but it did not prepare me to deal with the limitations on coping with their seemingly insatiable demands and confusion I felt in trying to set priorities among the main local church task. I felt surrounded by a sea of human need that I set out to fill through my own physical resources. My growing despair and anger occasionally surfaced in my sermons. I thought I was being prophetic, but actually I was berating them for not working as hard as I did. I was defenseless against the demands of ministry because I had no theological perspective for self-care and the management of my limitations. I had yet discovered what I meant to be a wounded healer.

During this time, there were many nights when I wished I could quit. Quitting seemed the only way out of my despair. One night sitting alone in the dark, I felt so lonely and empty that tears began to flow. My private communion set was on the coffee table. I wondered if I could find solace in giving myself communion, but rejected the idea with the thought that communion was only valid when celebrated within community. The Grace I preached to others I was unable to apply to myself. Many pastors caught in this kind of despair simply move on to another local church. If I had done that, I'm convinced I would have repeated the same patterns in a new place. What I needed was a whole new theology of ministry, one which included a theology of self-care.

The Kenosis of Christ

Jesus Christ is an excellent example of how to do ministry while taking care of oneself. Jesus didn't allow his caring to completely overextend him so that he had no energy for primary things. He offered himself as a sacrifice for the sake of the broken world, yet in spite of the magnitude of his mission he did not allow himself to get to strung out that he lost his center and his relationship with God. It was not that intent of the Gospel writers to show us how well Jesus took care of himself. Yet just look at some of the self-care passages that emerge in the Gospel narratives:

Mark 3:7; "*Jesus withdrew with his disciples to the sea...*"

Luke 9:10; "*One their return the apostles told him what they had done. And he took them and withdrew apart to the city called Bethsaida.*"

Luke 6:12; "*In these days he went out to the mountain to pray; and all night he continued in prayer to God.*"

Luke 5:15; "*But so much the more the report went aboard concerning him; and great multitudes gathered to hear and to be healed of their infirmities. But he withdrew to the wilderness and prayed.*"

Matthew 14:22; "*Then he made the disciples get into the boat and go before him to the other side, while be dismissed the crowds. And after he dismissed the crowds, he went up on the mountain by himself to pray. When the evening came he was alone...*"

The kenosis of Christ is his decision to empty himself for the sake of the world. He saw clearly the path he needed to take as the suffering servant spoken of in second Isaiah. This feature of Christ is best summed up in **Philippians 2:6-9** where the apostle Paul writes:

"CLERGY SELF CARE – FINDING A BALANCE FOR EFFECTIVE MINISTRY"

"...though he was in the form of God, did not count equality with God a thing to be grasped, but emptied himself, taking the form of a servant, being born in the likeness of [humans]/ And being fond in human form he humbled himself and became obedient unto death, even death on a cross."

From the time we need to be reminded that the redemption of the world has already been accomplished for us. Our own personal crucifixion will not add one iota to what Christ has already done for us.

Don't get it wrong. We still believe in a theology of the cross. The exercise of the cross for the clergy has to do with our call to be prophets, servants, and leaders in Christ's Church. There are times when we need to go to the mat on an issue, and if it means some people get upset with us or even leave the church, so be it. We must learn to choose our fights and stay healthy for the battles that really count.

Think about what would have become of Christ's mission if he had allowed himself to be continually exhausted by the poor and the sick, instead of dealing curtly with the Scribes and Pharisees, had allowed their questions and criticism to demoralize him. What if Jesus had allowed himself to be continually discouraged by the inability of his disciples to get to the point of his mission? What if he had become physically and emotionally exhausted, cynical, disillusioned, and self-deprecating? Would that have affected the course of history or influences your desire to commit our life to him?

Jesus chose kenosis rather than burnout, and because he did we are free to focus energy on primary issues in our churches. We do not need to be reduced to mush through burnout. Thomas Merton once said that we as clergy need to learn how to say 'no' to our people at times or else we will find ourselves supporting their illusions about ourselves and the world. As a pastor, I often found myself over-responding to every need, even the more neurotic ones. Since then I've learned that to be a person of compassion, I must not allow myself to become strung out with every human need that comes my way. I invite all of us to continue the struggle to become clearer about the difference between worthwhile priorities and those that merely deplete out energy and do not honor God.

NOTES

NOTES

CHAPTER 22

"Balancing The Demands of Ministry and Family" By; Michael Henderson

Introduction

Contemporary ministry is both rewarding and challenging at the same time. While the rewards are always welcomed, the impact of ministry challenges can prove to be harmful in many ways. If not careful, the pressures and demands of a life of service to others can result in great damage to the relationships that matter most; namely, the relationships that comprise the pastor's family and self. Since a health family-life is a prerequisite for pastoral ministry, as well as a safe-haven from hazards of ministry, the pastor's home must be his/her top priority.

> "As families in America grow weaker, so do an alarming number of pastor's families. However, Scripture establishes a strong, exemplary family as a prerequisite to pastoral ministry. Even-though the pressure in contemporary ministry is admittedly enormous, a marriage and family relationship characterized by the fruit of the Spirit and the love of Christ will be able to withstand the inevitable assaults of a pagan, postmodern culture and the intense demands of today's pastoral ministry. The pastor's home must be a top priority in his ministry."

I. The Biblical Benchmark
    a. 1 Timothy 3:2-5
    b. 1 Timothy 1:6

II. "WARNING! Ministry May Be Hazardous to Your Marriage."
    a. **A Pastoral survey discovered the following significant difficulties that led to marital problems in a pastoral home:**
        - 81% insufficient time together
        - 71% use of money
        - 70% income level
        - 64% communication difficulties

- 63% congregational expectations
- 57% differences in raising children
- 53% difficulty in raising children
- 46% sexual problems
- 41% pastor's unresolved anger issues
- 35% differences over ministry career
- 25% differences over spouse's career

b. **Additional statistical information (taken from Pastors at Greater Risk by H.B. London, Jr.)**
- 25% of pastor's wives see their husbands' work schedule as a source of conflict
- 13% of pastor's have been divorced
- Those in ministry are equally likely to have their marriage end in divorce as general church members
- The clergy has the second highest divorce rate among professions
- 24% of pastors have received marital counseling
- 80% of pastors say they have insufficient time with spouse
- 52% of pastors think being in ministry is hazardous to family well-being
- 21% of pastors wives want more privacy
- 45% of pastor's wives say the greatest danger to them and family is physical, emotional, mental and spiritual burnout
- 38% of pastor's wives say the number one frustration in ministry is time management
- 35% of pastor's report that their children's walk with God is the biggest concern about their families
- 41% of pastors say that the most stressful time of day in their home is evening
- 66% of pastors and their families feel pressure to model the ideal family to their congregations and communities

III. Balancing the Demands of Ministry and Family
   -Making the family a PRIORTY
   -The importance of being INTENTIONAL
   -The importance of ACCOUNTABILITY
   -Spending quality time (Building intimacy in the relationship)
   A. Dating your spouse
   B. Making time for your children (even adult children need time)
   C. The importance of getting in the world
   D. Learning their "Love Languages"

IV. Helpful Resources
   -Focus on the Family-FousontheFamily.com / Parsonage.org (Pastoral Care Division)
   -Family Life-FamilyLife.com

NOTES

Articles of Incorporation
Of
ABC-Church, Inc.
(A State Corporation)
Rex I. Frieze CPA

WHEREAS, it is deemed to be desirable and in the best interest of this church and its members that it be incorporated pursuant to the State Non-Profit Corporation Act, Chapter 123: now, therefore, be it:

RESOLVED, that the undersigned acting as incorporators of a State corporation under the State Non-Profit Corporation Act, Chapter 123, adopt the following Articles of Incorporation for such corporation.

Article I
Name and Location

The name of this corporation shall be ABC-Church, Inc. The street address of the principal location shall be: 1234 Straight Way, City, State 98765. The mailing address of this corporation shall be: P.O. Box 567, Straight Way, City, State 98765.

Article II
Duration

The corporation shall have perpetual existence and will commence on the filing of these articles by the Department of State.

Article III
Purpose

The purpose of ABC-Church is:

TO *exalt* the name of Jesus Christ through individual and corporate **worship** means

TO *equip* the saints for the works of the ministry through **instruction** means so the body may grow in the knowledge of the Son of God, to become mature disciples, and to fulfill the measure of the stature, which belongs to the fullness of Christ.

TO *edify* one another through **fellowship** means of encouraging one another and building up the Body into unity of faith.

TO *evangelize* our community, state, country, and world through **evangelism** means which proclaims the Word of God and calls everywhere to respond to Jesus Christ through faith.

TO *enable* the Body to fulfill this ministry purpose through the demonstration of wise **stewardship** over the resources God has so faithfully entrusted to this Body of Believers

This congregation is organized as a church exclusively for religious, charitable, and educational purposes within the meaning of Section 501 (c) (3) of the Internal Revenue Code of 1986 (or the corresponding provision of any future United States Internal Revenue law0 including, but not limited to, for such purposes, the establishing and maintaining of religious worship, the building, maintaining and operating of churches, parsonages, schools, colleges, chapels, radio stations, television stations, rescue missions, missionary auxiliaries, print shops, day care centers, camps, nursing retirement homes, cemeteries, and any other ministries that the elders of ABC-Church by providing opportunities for spiritual, physical, intellectual, social and cultural development.

Article VI
Initial Board of Directors

The names and addresses of the initial Board of Directors of the Corporation who will serve until the first election following incorporation are as follows:

John T. Smith	246 King Street, City, State 9855
Bill S. Care	357 Miller Way, City, State 98732
Ron C. Waters	864 Haskin Drive, City, State 98531
Susan W. Wave	890 South Street, City, State 98123
Jim A. Harris	471 Orange Avenue, City, State 98478

Article V
Initial Registered Office and Agent

The street address of the initial principal registered office of the corporation is: 1234 Straight Way, City, State 98765. The mailing address of the initial principal registered office of the corporation is: P.O. Box 567, Straight Way, City, State 98765. The name of the initial registered agent of the corporation at the address is: John T. Smith.

Article VI
Incorporators

The names and residence addresses of the subscribers of these Articles of Incorporation are the same as those in Article IV above.

Article VII
Tax-Exemption Provisions

No part of the net earnings of the Church shall inure to the benefit of or be distributed to its members, elders, officers, staff, or other private persons, except that the Church shall be authorized and empowered to pay reasonable compensation for the serviced rendered to make payments and distributions in furtherance of the purposes set forth in the Church's Constitution.

No substantial part of the activities of the Church shall be carrying on of propaganda or otherwise attempting to influence legislation. The Church shall not participate in, not intervene in (including the publishing or distribution of statements), and political campaign on behalf of any candidate for public office.

Article VIII
Conduct of Corporate Affairs

The conduct of the affairs of the Corporation will be limited as outlined in the Constitution and Bylaws of the Corporation. The powers of the Corporation are to be regulated as outlined in the constitution and Bylaws of the Corporation. The manner in which directors are elected or appointed will be as provided in the Bylaws of the Corporation.

Article IX
Dissolution of Corporate Affairs

If this Church should be dissolved, all of its assets remaining after payment of all outstanding debts and obligations, cost, and expenses of such dissolution shall be distributed to such non-profit organization or organizations organized and operated exclusively for religious purposes as shall at the time qualify as an exempt organization or organizations under Section 501 (c) (3) or the internal Revenue Code of 1986 or any regulations succeeding said Section. Asserts may be distributed only to organizations, which agree with the Church's Doctrinal Statement.

Members of said Church, defined in Bylaws, who are members in good standing at the time of the dissolution of the said Church, shall, in a called meeting, designate the religious organizations(s) to receive said assets of the Church after dissolution. None of the assets of said Church shall be distrusted to any member, elder, officer, or staff of this Church, or any individual.

Article X
Amendments of Article of Incorporation

The Articles of Incorporation may be amended by two-thirds (2/3) vote of those members present and voting when the members of the Corporation are meeting in conference as provided in the Bylaws of the Corporation.

Article XI
Qualifications For Membership

The qualification for membership in the Corporation and to serve as a director of the Corporation are stated in the Constitution and Bylaws of the Corporation. Directors shall be elected or appointed in accordance with the Constitution and Bylaws of the Corporation.

IN WITNES WHEREOF, the undersigned have executed these Articles of Incorporation this _____ day of _____, 2012

_____ _____
John T. Smith, Incorporator   Bill S. Care, Incorporator

_____ _____
Ron C. Waters, Incorporator   Susan W. Waters, Incorporator

_____
Jim A. Harris, Incorporator
STATE OF _____
COUNTY OF _____

BEFORE ME, the undersigned authority, authorized to take acknowledgements in the state and county set forth above, personally appeared:

JOHN T. SMITH, BILL S. CARE, RON C. WATERS, SUSAN W. WARE, AND JIM A. HARRIS, known to me and by me to be the persons who execute the foregoing Articles of Incorporation, and they acknowledge before me that they executed these Articles of Incorporation.

IN WITNESS WHEREOF, I have set my hand and affixed my official seal in the state and county aforesaid, this _____ day of _____, 2012.

_____
Notary Public, State of _____
My commission expires:

IMPORTANT NOTICE TO CHURCH LEADERS

This resource has been prepared solely for illustrative purposes. The resource is no intended to be all-inclusive with regard to laws and regulations and under no circumstances should it be relied upon for that purpose. Furthermore, because laws and regulations do frequently change and vary from one state to another, some materials in this resource may be outdated or not applicable. The services of competent accounting, legal, or other professional advisors should always be sought to review initial drafts and all final documents regarding those specific applications of professional standards, laws, and regulations that directly relate to your church.

Question: "What is the purpose of church by-laws (bylaws)?"
Answer: Most churches have a doctrinal statement, a document which condenses and systemizes the church's tenets of faith. A doctrinal statement is valuable in ensuring conformity to the Word of God and preventing the church from being 'tossed to and fro, and carried about by every wind of doctrine" (Ephesians 4:14). In addition to the articles of faith, most churches also have a set of by-laws (or bylaws), sometimes called the <u>rules of order</u> or a <u>constitution</u>. There are several practical reasons to have bylaws.

First, to promote efficiency, a church must have some type of organization. By-laws specify a church's governing structure; define the roles of pastor, elder, deacon, and other leaders; and stipulate the requirements for membership. In other words, bylaws allow "all things [to} be done decently and in order" (1 Corinthians 14:40).

Second to provide directions, a church needs to articulate its mission and methodology. The by-laws of a church are useful in setting parameters for fund raising, outreach, ordination, expenditures, and missionary support.

Third, to preserve unity and maintain its testimony, a church should agree on certain issues of Christian living and separation. A "gray area" which the Bible does not specifically address may be covered in a by-law. For example, a church may require its members to refrain from the consumption of alcohol; since this is not a doctrinal issue, per se, it is better dealt with in the by-laws.

Fourth, to protect itself from liability, a church should have written policies on church discipline, screening youth workers, etc. By-laws can be a way of averting calamity in crisis situation.

The following pages are sample bylaws for you to consider.

NOTES

BYLAWS
Of
ABC-Church, Inc.

A State Nonprofit Religious Corporation
Preamble to the Bylaws

ABC-Church endeavors to be a Church of the Lord Jesus Christ as described, and mandated by the New Testament. The purpose of these Bylaws is to help us accomplish the task of this Church in a "decent and orderly" manner through the use of effective and efficient means of good stewardship of the body's time, gifts and resources. Our ultimate desire is to bring glory to God through the Church.

These Bylaws are to provide general guidance on organization, governance and operation, based upon biblical principles and practices. However, the ultimate authority for ABC-Church's organization, governance and operation is the Bible. When a conflict or ambiguity exists with regard to these Bylaws, deference is to be given to the biblical reference to resolve the conflict or ambiguity.

Article I
Name and Principal Office

The name of the corporation is ABC-Church. This corporation will be further referred to in the Bylaws as the "Church" The Church maintains its principles office at 1234 Straight Way, City, State.

Article II
Membership

Section 1: General
The New Testament presents a picture of definable groups of who, once committed to the Lord, identified themselves with and committed themselves to a particular local body. (Rom. 16:1; 1 Cor. 1:2; 2 Cor. 8:1; Phil. 1:1; Acts 11:26)

In order to implement the principles of accountability and commitment to the local body of Christ, as defined in the New Testament and practiced in early churches, ABC-Church recognizes the need for formal membership. Membership in this Church shall consist of all persons who have met the qualities or membership and are listed on the membership role, after having completed.

Section 2: Candidacy and Membership

Any person 16 years of age or older who have personally received Christ as their Savior and Lord, who have receive baptism by immersion as testimony of their salvation, and who desire to be committed to ABC-Church as a local body of believers may become members of ABC-Church through the following procedures:

1. Approach an elder, staff member, deacon or other minister leader, or come forward during one of the worship service alter calls and share desire to join ABC-Church.
2. Attendance at New Membership Classes. Periodically, membership classes shall be offered to provide, but not limited to, the following:
    - o Introduction of elders and ministerial staff
    - o History of ABC-Church
    - o ABC-Church's Constitution (Philosophy of Ministry)
    - o Review of Bylaws
    - o Overview of ministries and insights from selected ministry leaders
    - o Spiritual gift studies
    - o General Operating Budget
    - o Leadership and membership responsibilities
3. Personal Interview
   Following attendance at New Membership Classes, individuals desiring membership shall meet with an elder or appointed ministry leader to verbalize their personal testimony, and to determine the integrity of their faith and their desire to be committed to ABC-Church as a local body of believers.
4. Signed Statement of Acknowledgment and Commitment
   A signed Statement of Acknowledgement and Commitment (Form No. 11-11) shall be used as an instrument to affirm one's desire for membership, to agree with the Church's covenant, and to serve as a formal record of one's membership.
   All such candidates shall be presents to this Church and membership by adding their names to the ABC-Church membership roll and publicizing their name and picture to the membership of ABC-Church in the Church's First Edition Publication.

Section 3: Designations of Membership

In an effort to properly reflect the membership of the church, two rolls shall be maintained. These rolls shall be updated periodically.

1. Active/Resident Members: All members who reside within the Church's ministry area or are currently active in the Church.
2. Nonresident Members: Members who have become inactive as a result of moving out of the Church's ministry area and have not joined another Church.

Section 4: Responsibilities of Membership

The responsibilities of membership are described in the Membership Covenant as documented in Church Constitution.

Each member shall sign a yearly Renewal of Membership Commitment (Form No. 11-15) to reaffirm his or her continued desire for membership. This recommitment shall include a brief description of how one is meeting the requirements of membership including, but not limited to, a:

1. Reaffirmation of one's commitment to ABC-Church's Constitution (Philosophy of Ministry) and Bylaws.
2. Description of how one is continuing to nurture his or her personal walk with Christ.
3. Reaffirmation of one's commitment to regular participation in corporate worship and fellowship of the Church.
4. Description of how one is stewarding his or her spiritual gifts, natural abilities and talents, and material resources to bring the greatest glory to God and the most benefit to people.

Section 5: Voting Rights of Membership

Every Active/Resident Member (except those members who are under the process of Church discipline, see Article II, Section 7) shall have the right o vote on the following matters:

- Adoption of the annual General Operating Budget of the Church
- Election of elders and deacons
- Acquisition of real property
- Disposition of all or substantially all of the assets of the Church
- Merger or dissolution of the Church
- Obtaining of any indebtedness
- Amendments to the Constitution, Articles of Incorporation ad Bylaws of the Church
- Calling or removing of the Senior Minister
- Other matters in which the Board of Elders feels led to seek the member's advice and counsel

Each Active/Resident Member of 16 years and older is entitled to one vote. Voting by proxy is prohibited.

All members may participate in the Lord's Supper ordinance of Church administered by the Church.

Section 6: Termination of Membership

Members shall be removed from the Church roll for following reasons:

1. Death
2. Transfer of Membership to another Church
3. By personal request of member
4. Dismissal by Senior Pastor according to a member's life and conduct which is not in accordance with the Church Membership Covenant and is in such a way that the member hinders the ministry influence of the Church in the community. Procedures are for the dismissal of a member shall be in accordance with Section 7 of this Article.

Section 7: Discipline of Members

Purpose: The purpose of Church discipline is to glorify God my maintaining (1) purity in the Church (1 Cor. 5:6), (2) protecting believers by deterring sin (1 Tim. 5:20) and (3) promoting the spiritual welfare of the offending believer by calling him or her to return to biblical standards of doctrine and conduct (Gal. 61). Furthermore, upon joining this church, all members are in agreement with Article VII (Binding Arbitration) of these Bylaws.

Process: Members and all other professing Christians who are regularly or fellowship at ABC-Church who err in biblical doctrine or conduct shall be subject to discipline according to Matthew 18:15-18. (Such person hereafter will be referred to as an "Erring Person".) Before such discipline reaches its final conclusion:

1. It shall be the duty of any Church member who has knowledge of the Erring Person's unbiblical beliefs or misconduct to warn and to correct such Erring Person in private, seeking his or her repentance ad restoration. If the Erring Person does not heed this warning; then,
2. The warning shall again go to the Erring Person accompanied by one or two witnesses to warn and correct such Erring Person, seeking his or her repentance and restoration. If the Erring Person still refuses to heed this warning; then,
3. It shall be brought to the attention of the Board of Elders. (It is understood that is process will continue to conclusion, whether the Erring person leaves ABC-Church or otherwise seeks to withdraw from membership to avoid the discipline process.) The elders will appropriately investigate any allegation brought by one Church member against another. If these allegations are warranted, two or more of the elders will contract Erring Person and seek his or her repentance and restoration. If the Erring Person refuses to be restored, the matter will be presented to the entire Board of Elders, who will act to protect the Church by removing the Erring Person's membership and notify the Church in accordance with Matthew 18. However, even at this point, ABC-Church will continue to pray for the restoration of the Erring Person and.

4. All claims or disputes, which cannot be resolved in accordance with Matthew 18 principles, shall be settled by biblically based and legally binding arbitration as set forth in Article VII of these Bylaws.

Reinstatement: If such dismissed member heeds to the warning, demonstrates repentance, and request reinstatement, he or she shall be publicly restored to membership through the affirmation of the Board of Elders and notification of ABC-Church membership.

Article III
Membership Meetings

Section 1: Place
Meeting of the members shall be held at a building on the Church property or at such other place or places within or outside the incorporated State as may be designated from time to time by the elders.

Section 2: General Meetings
A general meeting of the members shall be held in January of each year at such a time as determined by the elders. This general meeting shall be annual membership meeting. The purpose of this meeting shall be to adopt an annual General Operating Budget and to elect any new elders. Subject to Section 4 of this Article, and other proper business may be conducted at this meeting.

Section 3: Special Meetings
Special meeting may be called at any time by the Senior Pastor/Elders for any purpose by giving a notice to the members in accordance with Section 4 of this Article.

Section 4: Notice Requirements for Membership Meetings
General Requirements: Whenever members are required or permitted to take any action at a meeting, notice shall be given to members no less than two (2) weeks prior to a meeting. Notification of membership meeting shall be given in any of the following manners, which shall be deemed to be reasonable method of calling a membership meeting:

1. Distribution of written materials to the congregation in attendance at a regular weekend worship service
2. Announcement of the meeting in the Church Newsletter
3. Oral Announcement to the congregation at a mid-week worship service
4. Delivery by United States mail to each member identified on the membership roll

Notice of Certain Agenda Items: Action by the members on any of the following proposals, other than by unanimous approval by those members present and entitle to vote, it valid only if the notice or wavier of notice specifies the general nature of the proposal:

1. Selection, rebuke, or dismissal of the Senior Minister
2. Amending the Articles off Incorporation
3. Adopting, amending or repealing the Bylaws
4. Disposing of all substantially all of the Church's assets
5. Approving the acquisition of real property and related indebtedness
6. Approving the election to dissolve the Church

Section 5: Quorum
Those members present and voting at a meeting duly noticed and called shall constitute a quorum of membership for the transaction of business.

Section 6: Voting
Church action shall be by concurrence of majority of members present and voting, except for calling or removal of the Senior Minister which shall require an affirmative vote of three-fourths (3/4) of those present and voting, and the amending of the constitution, Articles of Incorporation and Bylaws which shall be by those physically present at the Church meeting at which a vote is taken and no proxy votes shall be allowed.

Section 7: Rule of Order
Except where Bylaws state otherwise, Robert's Rules of Order shall be the accepted pattern for the transaction of all Church Business. The Elders shall retain the right to appoint a parliamentarian to help in all Church meetings.

The Moderator for all Church meeting shall be the Senior Pastor and or/Chairman of the Board of Elders. In the absence of the Chairmen of Elders the Vice-Chairman of Elders will serve as the Moderator. The Senior Minister will always be allowed to Speak in Church meeting if he so elects.

The Corporate Secretary will be responsible for recording the minutes of the meeting. The minutes should include who presided over the meeting; quorum of members, summary of actions taken at the meeting but sufficient detail to clearly describe what was discussed and agreed upon to avoid any subsequent disputes.

Church meeting are open to any Church member desiring to attend. Visitors and non-members will be dismissed before meetings commence.

Article IV
Board of Elders

Section 1: General Scope

ABC-Church seeks to be a New Testament Church committed to the teachings of the Bible. No other authority or tradition is to guide the means, faith, or structure of the Lord Jesus Christ's Church. The Pastoral and administrative structure for a New Testament Church is to utilize a plurality/team form of leadership. ABC-Church will follow this scriptural example.

To achieve this New Testament model, ABC-Church requires qualified men to sere on the Board of Elders. These men must be specific moral and spiritual qualifications before they can serve. Selection will be based on biblical directives such as: character (1 Tim.:1-10), giftedness (1 Cor.12:12-31), function (Romans 12:3-8) and results (Eph. 4:11-16). They must be publicly installed into office (1 Tim.5:22; Acts 14:23). They must be motivated and empowered by the Holy Spirit to do their works of ministry (Acts 20:28). After review, examination, and appointment, as described in this Section, men affirmed by ABC-Church to serve as elders shall constitute the "Board of Elders". To effectively perform their duties, the Board of Elders needs the prayers, support (1 Tim. 5:17-18) and assent of members of ABC-Church (Heb. 13:17). ABC-Church is called upon to honor their Board of Elders and to protect them against false accusations (1 Tim. 5:19). Finally, if an elder falls into sin, and continue is sin, he must be publicly rebuke (1 Tim. 5:20)

The government of this Church, under the leadership of the Holy Spirit, shall be vested in the Board of Elders (except in matters reserved to the members, as defined in these bylaws). The elders shall be elected as provided in the articles of those Bylaws, and the elders shall appoint corporate officers and directors. While the scriptures indicates that elders bear the ultimate responsibility for the watch care of the Church, and Executive Council will establish by the Board of Elders and authority specifically delegated by the elders to this Council to oversee legal and financial matters and provide for the care and maintenance of all properties owned by ABC-Church As necessary, further delineation of responsibilities shall be determined jointly by the elders and the Execution Council. The membership of the Board of Elders, the elders' duties, their terms of office, and other qualities shall be as follows:

Sections 2: Qualifications and Discipline

"An overseer then must be above reproach, the husband of one wife, temperate, prudent, respectable, hospitable, able to teach, not addicted to wine or pugnacious, but gentle, uncontentious, and free from the love of money. He must be one who manages his own household well, keeping children under control with all dignity...and not a new convert, he must have a good reputation with those outside the Church, so he may not fall into reproach and at the snare of the devil." 1 Tim. 3:2-7

"If a man be above reproach, the husband of one wife, having children who believe, not accused of dissipation or rebellion...above reproach as God's steward, not self-willed, not quick-tempered, not addicted to wine, not pugnacious, not fond of sordid gain, but hospitable, loving what is good, sensible, just, devout, self-controlled, holding fast the faithful word...that he may be able to both exhort in sound doctrine and refute those who contradict.

Above Reproach - Elders must be blameless, presenting no patterns of Scriptural disobedience or grounds for accusation.

Husband of One Wife – Elders, if married, must be devoted spouses.

Temperate – Elders must be self-controlled, enslaved to nothing, free from excesses.

Prudent – Elders must be sober, sensible, wise, balanced in judgment, not given to quick, superficial decisions based on immature thinking.

Respectable – Elders must demonstrate a well-ordered life and good behavior.

Hospitable – Elders must be unselfish with their personal resources. They must be willing to share blessing with others.

Able to Teach – Elders must be able to communicate the truth of God and exhort sound doctrine in a non-argumentative way. (II Tim. 4:2 & 2:24)

Not Addicted to Wine – Elders must be free from addictions, and must be willing to limit their liberty for the sake of others.

Not Pugnacious – Elders must be gentle and characterized by forbearance and tenderness – not having a quick temper.

Uncontentious – Elders must not be given to quarreling or selfish arguments.

Free From the Love of Money – Elders must not be stingy, greedy or out for sordid gain. They should not be preoccupied with amusing material things, but rather should be a model of giving.

Manage Own Household – Elders must have a well-ordered household, a healthy family life, and well-behaved children. (Pertains to those children still under the authority of the parents).

Not a New Covert – Elders must not be new believers. They must have been Christians for long enough to demonstrate the reality of their conversion and the depth of their spirituality.

NOTE: Suggested guideline-at least two years from the time of ABC-Church Membership.

Good Reputation with Outsiders – Elders must be well respected by unbeliever, and must be free from hypocrisy.

Not Self-Willed – Elders must be stubborn, insensitive or prone to force opinions on others. They must be more interested in service than self-pleasure.

Not Quick Tempered – Elders must be able to exercise self-control and patience in difficult situations.

Loves what is Good – Elders must desire the will of God in every decision.

Just – Elders must be fair and impartial. Their judgment must be based on Scriptural principles.

Devout – Elders must be reverent, continually desiring to be separated from sin. They must be devoted to prayer, the study of Scripture and the guarding of their own spiritual walk. (Acts 20:28)

Holding Fast the Faithful Word – Elders must be stable in faith, obedient to the word of God, continually seeking to be controlled by the Holy Spirit.

It is the Elder Board's responsibility to discipline or remove any Board member who no longer fulfills the qualifications of an elder, who fails to fulfill his responsibilities, or who violates the intent of the Bylaws. Discipline or removal shall be by a three-fourths (3/4) vote of all elders (except the elder being discipline or removed).

The Senior Minister of the ministerial staff shall be voting member of the Board of Elders. He will represent the interest of ministerial and support staff of the Church. All other ministerial staff personnel cannot be members of the Board, even though they meet the qualifications for an elder.

Section 3: Duties

It is the elders' duty to exercise personal holiness. Elders shall oversee, lead, shepherd, and care for the spiritual condition of the Church, as set forth in Scripture (I Timothy 5:17; Titus 1:9; I Peter 5:1-2). The Board of Elders can delegate selected ministry oversight to appointed Ministries Council.

Specific List of Responsibilities:

1. Shepherd the Flock. Serving in all humility, elders are to guide, direct, guard ad protect the members of the body, seeking to meet their needs and to assist in any way possible, warning against harmful influences and guarding against false teachers. (Acts 20:35)
2. Lead Through Example. Elders are to provide a Scriptural role model and re to set a pattern before the flock of a rightly ordered life-with a single purpose, to glorify God. (1 Timothy 3:4-5; 5:17)
3. Teach and Exhort. Elders are to see that the flock is fed through insightful and accurate Biblical instruction and admonition. Teaching will be centered on equipping the members of the body to perform works of Ministry. (1 Timothy 3:2; Titus 1:9-26; John 21:17)
4. Refute Those Who Contradict Truth. Elders are to confront those who are teaching what they should not teach or who are continuing in a pattern of behavior contradictory to Biblical truth. Thus, elders are to keep closing potential entrances for Satan, so that the truth of Christ will remain creditable to both the congregation and the community. (Acts 20:17, 28-31; 1 Thess 5:12)
5. Manage the Church of God. Elders are to oversee the life of the Church, with the assistance of other godly leaders. They must be people who can "rule well". Deacon

qualified men are to be selected to assist the elders in the management and ministry of the Church. (I Timothy 5:17)
6. Pray for the Sick. Elders are to pray for the spiritual and physical wellbeing of members of the congregation. (James 5:14-15)

Elders, like the Church members, have no individual authority but must act together as a board to represent the best interest of the Church. All board actions are authorized by the elders passing a "resolution." The Board of Elders has complete authority to govern the secular areas of the Church, except in matters that are either delegated to Executive Council as noted above, or reserves to vote of the Church membership. The elders may also establish various advisory committees to assist them in both administrative and ministry matters.

The Board of Elders has the authority—by a majority vote of its members present and voting at a meeting at which quorum is present—to hire, select, dismiss, and have salaries set for all ministerial staff positions. The congregation has authority to hire, select and dismiss the Senior Minister. All other support staff positions shall be hired, selected, dismissed, and have their salaries set by recommendation from the Senior Minister and Personnel Committee.

The Board of Elders shall have any other and responsibilities that are described in these Bylaws.

Sections 4: Election and Indefinite Terms of Service
While the Bible does not give instruction as to the number of elders a Church should have, it is recognized that there must be plurality. Therefore, both the number of elders annually elected and the number of elders serving on the Board of Elders at any one time shall be unlimited. The Holy Spirit shall call specific men to serve as elders and we will consider these men adequate to serve as our Board of Elders.

Each elder, upon appointment, shall be asked for one-year commitment, subject to review, recommitment and re-affirmation by the Church members each year. During the period of annual review, both the individual and the other elders shall evaluate his continued service as an elder, again considering the Biblical qualifications as well as any personal factors that might affect his service. An individual's service as an elder may be discontinued by his own decision, or by the unanimous decision of the other elders.

Those elders renewing their annual commitment would again be presented to the Church members of affirmation and dedication. A person's leaving the Board of Elders would not preclude his service as a future elder, subject to the regular selection process.

Men who aspire to be elders, due to calling of God, should express that desire to an elder of ABC-Church. The process for selecting new elders in outline in Selection 8 of this Article.

Section 5: Vacancy
If any vacancy occurs on the Board of Elders, the vacancy may be filled by three-fourths (3/4) vote of the members of the Elder Board. The man selected to fill the vacancy shall serve until

the next Annual Meeting. Elders can take leaves of absence and be reinstated to active service as described in the Bylaws.

Section 6: Oversight and Election of Corporate Officers
Annually, the Board of Elders will elect the corporate officers to serve on the Executive Council of the Church. These officers represent the Chairman, Vice-Chairman, Treasurer, and Secretary.

These men shall act as the administrative officers of both the Board Elders and the Corporation. The officers shall all be under the control and direction of the Board of Elders. As administrative officers of the corporation, they shall have the same duties and responsibilities as the same officials in a corporation formed for profit. They may also have other duties as directed or delegated by the Board of Elders or by these Bylaws. Active elders will serve as the directors of the Corporation.

These administrative officers shall function as the trustees of ABC-Church. They manage ABC-Church property, both real and personal, as fiduciaries. They shall represent ABC-Church in all of its legal matters. They will directly report to the Board of Elders and make periodical reporting to the Board. At least one elder, who has spiritual gift administration, will serve on the Executive Council.

Each elder maintains the right to nominate a fellow Board member as an officer. The elders will receive council from members of the existing Executive Council as to other possible nominees. All corporate officer nominees must meet deacon qualifications. All nominations should be submitted to the Nomination Committee four weeks to the meeting at which the election will take place.

The Nominating Committee members will meet with each nominee meets deacon qualification and is willing to accept the position, should they be elected. The committee will report back to the board of Elders with its findings. The Elders will vote on the nominees for the upcoming fiscal year.

At no time should the Senior Minister or any other employee serve as a corporate officer of the Church.

If, for any reason, an elected officer cannot fulfill the duties of the office for the entire year, the elders will once again be asked to submit nominations. The Nomination Committee will have two weeks to meet with each nominee to determine the nominee's willingness to accept the position, should they be elected. The committee will then report its findings to the elders at their next meeting, during which a formal vote will be taken.

Refer to Article V, Section 6 as to corporate officers of the Executive Council.

Section 7: Meeting and Quorum
The Board of Elders will hold monthly meeting at a time and place decided by the Board. The Annual Meeting of the Board will correspond with the Church Annual meeting. A quorum for Elder Board meeting shall consist of two-thirds (2/3) of the voting members. For

approval of any matters before the Board, a majority vote of those members of the Board who present, at which a quorum is present, shall be necessary unless specified elsewhere in these Bylaws.

Section 8: Nomination of Elders
Scriptures gives evidence of the first elders being appointed by the founders of the Church. By this example it is implied that the existing spiritual leadership of a church can be intimately involved in the process of selecting elders, so as to ensure that the selection process is based on spiritual rather than superficial qualifications.

In September of each year, the elders currently serving shall determine the number of positions, if any, to be filled that year on the Board of Elders. If the elders determine that additional elders are needed, they shall initiate following process for elder selection:

1. The existing shall appoint a nominating Committee consisting of at least three members, none of who currently serve as an elder of currently, aspire to be elder. Each member of this committee shall meet deacon qualifications. For the purpose of order, one member of the Nominating Committee shall be chosen by the committee as chairman of the committee.
2. The Nominating Committee will meet with the elders to review the qualifications for elders and determine questions that should be posted to the candidates.
3. The congregation shall be provided with teaching regarding qualifications for elders and their Spiritual role.
4. With the Biblical qualifications in mind, members of the congregation will be given <u>30 days</u> to submit prayerfully the names of male members for consideration as elders.
5. Men whose names are submitted shall be so informed, and they shall be urged to engage in self-appraisal and personal evaluation in light of the Scriptural qualifications. Any purpose may withdraw his name at that point, if he does not aspire to the position of elder (1 Tim. 3:1) or if he does not believe he adequately meets the qualifications or has the time to serve.
6. The Nominating Committee shall review the names of the nominees, and shall conduct interviews with each nominee. Consideration will be given as to the present Board of Elder's spiritual gift mix and talents. It is the desire of the elders to lead the Church with mean who have diverse gifts and talents.
7. After prayerfully considering each nominee, the Nominating committee shall make final recommendations to the elders. Those nominees who have not been recommended to the elders shall be informed by the committee as to the reason for their being recommended, with reference to whatever qualifications might have been fulfilled.
8. The elders shall review the nominees and make a final selection. Nominees not selected at this point shall also be given reason by the elders as to why they were not selected.

9. The names of prospective elders shall be brought before the members of the church, who will be given 30 days to show cause why any of the prospective elders would be qualified to serve. Consistent with Matt. 18:15 and Matt. 5:24, any member with such "cause" must first express his concern to the prospective elder and then must also express his concern to the Board of Elders for consideration.
10. At the end of the 30-day period, the prospective elders will be presented to the members of the Church for affirmation by majority vote of the members present, and for a service of dedication. Such time of affirmation and dedication shall occur every year, whether to affirm new elders, or re-affirm the service of existing elders.

The whole process of selection shall begin in September of each year, and take three to four months. In the event of vacancy of special need, the elders may refer to previous nominees to make a selection or may re-initiate the whole selection process, as they deem necessary

It is recognized that most all ABC-Church ministers will meet elder qualifications, but due to the need for uncompromised levels of spiritual authority, the Senior Minister will serve on the Board of Elders as the only staff elder being accountable for and representative of all staff positions. No other ministerial or support staff person can serve as a member of the Board of Elders. However, their presence can be requested for elder meetings. Furthermore, not more than one member of a family of the Church or one participant in a close personal relationship shall serve on the Board of Elders at any given time.

As stated in Section 4 of this Article, each elder, upon appointment, shall be asked for a one-year commitment, subject to review, recommitment and re-affirmation by the church members each year. This annual appointment will be made part of the annual membership, which is held in January of each year.

Article V
Church Leadership

Section 1: Overview of Church Leadership
The Board of Elders has final authority over all matters of ABC-Church. The Senior Ministry has responsibility over all paid staff of the Church. Deacons will assist the elders in meeting ministry and administrative needs of the Church ad they arise. The Executive Council will oversee legal and financial matters and provide for the care and maintenance of all properties owned by ABC-Church. The Ministries Council will serve as the overseer to the numerous ministries of ABC-Church. Committees and Ministry Teams will be established to perform works of administration or ministry as outlined in their specific Position Descriptions.

Section 2: Senior Minister
Duties of the Senior Minister As mentioned in Article IV, Section 8 of these Bylaws, the Senior Minister will serve on the Board of Elders as the only staff elder, being accountable for and a

representative of all staff positions. Compensation paid to the Senior Minister by ABC-Church is for services rendered as the Senior Minister of the Church and is not to be considered for services rendered as an elder of the Board. The Senior Minister's service on the Board of Elders is considered voluntary and non-compensatory.

In addition to his pastoring role as an elder, the Senior Minister is primarily to be a teacher of the Word of God—the Bible. He is to teach and exhort by precept and example. His goal is to help mature believers through insightful and accurate presentation and proclamation of the Word, equipping them to effectively perform works of ministries within the Body of Christ. Thus, the Senior Minster should not be responsible to the minister in areas unrelated to his primary function as a teaching and equipping elder. To burden the Senior Minister with other functions (i.e. administration, counseling, visitation, etc.) to rod him of study time and devotion to the Word. As shepherds of the Church, it is one of the roles of the Board of Elders to appoint other leaders with complementary gifts to undertake areas and aspects of the ministry and cannot and should not be filled by the Senior Minister. Senior Minister should possessor be registered to receive a Master of Divinity Degree (minimally), and preferably be a pastoral degree holder.

The Senior Minster is also responsible as a member of the Board of Elders to lead the Church to function as a New Testament Church and ultimately achieve its mission and ministry objectives. This individual is to give oversight direction and leadership to the ministries of ABC-Church. As such, he will work closely with the Ministries and Executive Councils and Church staff. The Senior Minister shall be an ex officio member of all councils, committees and ministry teams, and his leadership shall be recognized in all of them. The Board of Elders will prepare a Position Description for the Senior Minister, which outlines more specific responsibilities and duties.

Election of Senior Minster The Senior Minister shall be chosen and called by the Church whenever a vacancy occurs. His election shall take place at a Church meeting called specifically for the purpose.

Minister Search Committee When a vacancy in the senior pastorate exists; a Minister Search Committee shall be established with Church membership approval. The search committee will be responsible for screening all resumes, interviewing applicants, and confirming the qualifications and experience of top candidates. The Board of Elders will be consulted during the search process. Their recommendation will constitute nomination.

The Minister Search Committee will be comprised of the Chairman of the Board of Elders, Chairman of the Deacon Fellowship, Chairperson of the Missions Ministry Team, Chairperson of the Personnel Committee, Chairperson of the Finance Committee, and four (4) members elected at large by the Church in a special called Church meeting. Two (2) alternatives will be chosen for any reason a vacancy occurs.

Once the Minister Search Committee has selected a candidate, that candidate shall be presented to the Executive Council, Ministries Council, ministerial staff, and deacons for affirmation by a two-thirds (2/3) vote of those present. If a positive affirmation is obtained, the committee will then bring their recommendation to the Church members; the affirmation vote, by written ballot, of three-fourths (3/4) of those present is necessary for an affirmed choice of the Senior Minister. The Senior Minister, thus elected, shall serve until the relationship is terminated by his or the Church's requested pursuant to the following section.

Once the Minister Search Committee has selected a candidate to fill the Senior Minister position, the Personnel Committee will enter into contract negotiations with the candidate based on directives from the Board of Elders.

The Senior Minister's call will detail annual evaluation process. It will also identify specific ministry objectives for the church and detail information related to compensation, fringe benefits, authority and responsibility.

Tenure of Office of Senior Minister The tenure of the office of Senior Minister may be terminated at any time by the Senior Minister of the Church. If the Senior Minster relinquishes the office, he may do so by giving at least four (4) weeks' notice at the time of resignation.

The Church may declare the office of Senior Minister to be vacant if circumstances dictate. Such action shall take place at a meeting called for that purpose, with at least a two (2) week's written notice given to all members. The meeting may be called only upon the recommendation of two-thirds (2/3) of the Board of Elders and three-fourths (3/4) of the Deacon Fellowship or by written petition signed by not less than one-third (1/3) of the resident Church members. The moderator of this meeting shall be the Chairman of the Elders or, in his absence, the Vice-Chairman of the Elders. The vote to declare the office of Senior Minster vacant shall be by written ballot with three-fourths (3/4) affirmation vote of those present.

Section 3: Other Ministerial Staff
Ministers (excluding the Senior Minister) are called to serve by the recommendation from the Board of Elders and are empowered by the elders for running the day-to-day ministry operations of the Church. Ministers can act individually to enter into transaction regarding their specific area of ministry, conditioned upon budgetary constraints, but they are subject to the oversight of the Board of Elders and authorization levels given to them by the Senior Minister and the Board. If a minister exceeds his or her authorization level in a church transaction, the minister may be held personally responsible for any obligations incurred as a result. The Senior Minister is responsible, and will be held accountable to the Board of Elders, for the oversight of all ministerial staff of the Church.

Position Descriptions shall be written when the need for a staff member is determined. All ministerial staff members will be required to meet deacon qualifications, regardless of their specific area of ministry. When a ministerial position is to be established or filled, a Minister

Search Committee shall be established consisting of two (2) members of the Ministries Council, one (1) members of the Board of Elders, one (1) members from the Personnel Committee, one (1) member from the Finance Committee, and two (2) members-at-large, selected from the Church membership by the Nominating Committee, Recommendations will be presented to the Board of Elders for their approval. New ministerial staff positions will be introduced to the membership of the Church.

Section 4: Support Staff
The oversight of support staff members will be performed by the Minister of Administration in consultation with the Senior Minister. Guidelines for the hiring and termination of support staff positions are documented in the Personnel Section of the Policies and Procedures Manual.

Section 5: Deacon Fellowship
General Scope Deacons are the servant-ministers of the Church. Their purpose is to relieve the elders of the multitude of practical duties of caring for the flock. No specific, on-going deacon roles are mentioned in the Scripture, probably because service needs change, and so the role of the deacons must remain flexible. Perhaps this is why qualifications for deacons are stressed in Scripture rather than specific tasks. Deacons are to give their primary attention toward caring for the congregation's physical welfare. Deacons have the honor of modeling, for the local Church and the lost world, God's compassion, kindness, mercy, and love. As the Church compassionately cares for people's needs, the world sees a visible display of Christ's love, which will draw some people to the Savior. Deacons are to be an example of commitment, unity, and harmony in their service.

Their primary service will consist of giving administrative oversight to Standing Committees or ministry oversight to Ministry Teams, which have been established by the elders. Examples of specific service would be: the collectors of funds, the distributors of relief, and agents of mercy. They help the poor the jobless, the sick, the widowed, the elderly, the homeless, the shut-in, and the disabled. They comfort, protect, and encourage, and help to meet their needs. Although they do in many ways meet spiritual needs of those whom they serve, their primary service is related to physical needs.

Number, Election, Terms of Office The Deacon Fellowship shall consist of twenty-five (25) or more active Deacons. Deacons shall be elected by the Church at the annual Church Meeting. The Deacons so elected shall take office on January 1 following their election and shall serve on a three (3) year rotational basis. There is no obligation to constitute as an active Deacon a person who comes to the Church from another congregation where he served as an active Deacon.

Rotation The term of office of Deacons shall expire on December 31 of their third (3rd) year of service. After serving as a Deacon, no man shall be eligible to serve another term until the lapse of at least on (1) year.

Qualifications Any man who is a member of the Church over twenty-five (25) years of age and meets the qualifications of Scripture shall be eligible for the office of Deacon, provided he is willing and able to serve. He shall also have been an active member of the church for a period of at least one (1) year at the time of his election. Any many joining ABC-Church by profession of faith shall have been an active member of this Church for a period of at least two (2) years at the time of election.

He shall also meet the qualifications of Acts 6:3 and 1 Timothy 3:8-13. His duties are Church wide, covering areas of need, ministry, soul winning, etc. It is his duty to be a positive encouragement in all matters concerning the welfare of the Church, but it is understood that he does not have authority over the Church, except when that authority has been delegated by the Board of Elders. The Deacons Fellowship will be the primary pool of spiritually qualified individuals who the elders will use to assist them in meeting ministry and administrative needs of the church as they arise. Each Deacon must be supportive of the elders, Senior Minister, staff, and ministry philosophy of ABC-Church.

Section 6: Executive Council

General Overview While Scripture indicated that elders bear the ultimate responsibility for the watch care of the Church it does allow for the delegation of responsibilities. Therefore, the elders of ABC-Church have specifically delegated to the Executive Council the responsibility of overseeing the legal, financial, business and executive matters of the Church. This Council will also oversee all Standing Committees and provide for the care and maintenance of all properties owned by ABC-Church. Members of the Executive Council also serve as the corporate officers of the Church as so noted in Article 4, Section of these Bylaws. The Executive Council is accountable to the Board of Elders.

The Executive Council shall create whatever internal organization it deems appropriate to carry out its responsibilities and to fulfill any requirements necessary for them to act as legal representatives of ABC-Church. For the purpose of coordination and communication, the Executive Council shall include elder representation.

Specific List of Responsibilities:

1. To assist the Board of Elders and the Senior Minister in the administrative oversight of the Church. To determine and ensure that all of the administrative committee of the Church are performing their designated responsibilities.

2. Provide oversight for all legal, financial and executive related committees. Review and update the fiscal policies and procedures and responsibilities of these committees.
3. Perform and maintain a fiduciary responsibility to the church in all legal, financial and executive matters
4. Review and make recommendations for Bylaws and Articles of Incorporation revisions.
5. Executive all legal documents relative to contracts, church property and other business matters as conditioned by these bylaws.
6. Participate in strategic planning of the Church.

Corporate Officer Positions and Responsibilities:

Chairman: The Chairman sets goals and objectives for Executive Council that assist and compliment the Board of Elder's vision and purpose statements and ministry goals. The Chairman recommends needed administrative committees, and is responsible for assigning work and overseeing its completion on a timely basis. The Chairman presides over Council meetings and is responsible for preparing meeting agendas and leading such meetings. This person will also regularly attend elder meetings when requested and keep the Board apprised as to the operational integrity of the Church.

Vice-Chairman: The Vice-Chairman will serve in the absence of the Chairman and perform other duties delegated by the Chairman.

Treasurer: The Treasurer presents monthly financial reports at Council meetings and keeps the Council informed regarding the general operating budget. The Treasurer, together with the Finance committee and the Minister of Administration, assists in managing the Church's investment portfolio and reviews all investment transactions for appropriateness. This person is responsible for working closely with the Finance Committee Chairman and the Minister of Administration to ensure high level of fiscal integrity over the financial affairs of the church. This individual is also responsible for providing a monthly financial reporting to the Board of Elders.

Secretary: The Secretary takes minutes of Council meetings and mails them to Council members on timely basis. A staff person could be selected to perform this task. This would allow the secretary to more fully participate in Council proceedings. It is the responsibility of the Secretary to review all minutes of the Board of Elders, Executive council and administrative committees under the Executive Council's oversight. These minutes will be reviewed for accuracy and completeness before they are filed in the church office as permanent records. The Secretary will be responsible for maintaining these minutes in an orderly manner and retrieving such information when needed. This individual will also be required to take minutes of all congregational meetings and maintain secure accurate membership information for the purpose of determining quorums. The Secretary must be familiar with *Robert's Rules of Order* since he/she acts as the Council's parliamentarian.

The Secretary may prepare correspondence on behalf of the Executive Council, execute corporate papers, serve as the council's notary and perform other assigned duties.

All legal instruments that must be signed for the Corporation shall be signed by the Chairman or Vice-Chairman, sealed with corporate seal, attested to by the Secretary.

Section 7: Ministries Council
General Overview The Ministries Council is responsible for the oversight of all ministries and Ministry Teams of ABC-Church. Chairpersons of the various Ministry Teams will compose this Council. The Ministries Council is accountable to the Board of Elders. The ministers Council is composed of four ministry emphases of ABC-Church s noted in the Constitution. They are:

- Worship Team (Exaltation)
- Instruction Team (Equipping) Fellowship Team (Encouragement)
- Evangelism Team (Evangelization)

Specific List of Responsibilities

1. Coordinate and evaluate all ministry programs of the Church.
2. Establish the church ministry calendar each year.
3. Recommend Church ministry objectives and goals.
4. Recommend and evaluate changes in Ministry Teams.

Section 8: Standing Committees
General Scope Committees can be established by the Board of Elders. The Purpose for establishing committees is to assist the elders and staff in doing the administrative works of ministry in a "decent and orderly" manner. Committees will possess certain authority and responsibility levels of the corporate Church as delegated by the Board of Elders. Each approved committee will function under a Ministry Position Description. This description will outline their purpose and that duties and responsibilities have been delegated to the Committees' functions will be primarily administrative in nature versus ministry Teams whose primary functions are ministry in nature. Individual's serving on these committees will be selected by Nominating Committee, which has been established by the Board of Elders. Each chairperson of a Standing Committee will serve on the Executive Council. Spiritual giftedness will be primary qualification for service. The leadership of ABC-Church feels that committees should be held to a minimum. The present Standing Committees of ABC-Church are as follows:

- Finance Committee
- Personnel Committee
- Facilities Committee
- Legal Committee
- General Administration Committee

Additional supporting committees can be established by the Executive Council to assist the various Standing Committees. The Organizational Manual of the Church discloses all Standing and supporting Committees and their appropriate Ministry Position Descriptions.

Election Elections of committee members may be conducted in more than o0ne (1) session. Regular elections shall be completed prior to January 1. Special elections may be held as needed. Person elected at regular elections shall begin their service on January immediately following their election, unless otherwise stated. Persons elected at special elections shall begin their ministry as soon as they are elected unless some other time is stated at the time of election.

Rotation Election of active committee members shall be based on the principle of a three (3) year rotation system, with a three (3) year term and a one (1) year minimum gap in service. Ideally, one-third (1/3) of the members each year would be elected to three (3) year terms.

Unexpired terms When a position is vacated prior to completion of the elected term, a person is to be elected to complete the unexpired position of the term. He or she may be eligible foe a new three (3) year term upon completion of serving the unexpired term.

Enlarged Membership When the size of the active committees is increased, one-third (1/3) of the additional members are elected for a one (1) year term, one-third (1/3) for a two (2) year term, one-third (1/3) for a three (3) year term. Fractional terms will exist when members are added at times other than for January 1 assumption of service.

Eligibility to Serve Consecutive Terms:

1. Persons completing a full three (3) year regular term will not be nominated or re-elected to the same position until a one (1) year waiting period has passed. The one (1) year waiting does not affect service in other positions.
2. Persons completing a partial term, but having less than three (3) years consecutive service on the same committee, may be re-elected to term of three (3) years or less, without a one (1) year waiting period.
3. Members may have one (1) year waiting requirements waived when the Board of Elders votes to do so.
4. Members of the same immediate family many not serve on the same committee simultaneously.

Section 9: Ministry Teams

Ministry Teams exist to perform a specific role of ministry. Teams perform ministry best when they are performed by plurality. Teams are the basic organizing units of ABC-Church of accomplish its ministry goals within the guidelines of our Purpose Statement. These teams devise and carry out the numerous ministries of ABC-Church. Unlike, committees, their primary role is no to exercise administrative responsibilities or set policy. Ministry teams will possess no authority or responsibility levels if the corporate Church and are not subject to any service rotation system. Rather they, are the "hands and feet" of the body of Christ. A team is a small group of people with complementary skills committed to a common purpose or goal and for which they are willing to be mutually accountable. Teams are an effective way to help people identify their spiritual gifts and to empower them with a passion for ministry. Teams may exist for a very short term to perform a specific ministry or may be on going in nature. On-going Ministry Team will be enlisted for one year of service and re-enlisted as needed every year. Ministry Teams may carry in size depending upon their specific purpose and upon those available to serve in that capacity. The appropriate staff representative shall recruit them with the assistance of the Nominating Committee as needed. Each Ministry Team will function under a Ministry Position Description, which will outline their primary ministry purpose and briefly describe anticipated duties and responsibilities. Unlike committee ministry position Descriptions their duties are not required. However, leadership still feels that such descriptions are needed so as to assure that the ministry function is in fact fulfilling ABC-Church's purpose statement and ministry objectives and goals. The Ministerial Staff shall give overall supervision to all teams and oversee the selection of team leaders. Each Ministry Team leader is required to serve on the Ministries Council. This is because each ministering part of the body needs to be connected to the entire body (Ephesians 4:16) as to allow for effective communication and an avenue which allows for input to and from the Board of Elders and staff. Examples of several Ministry Teams are as follows:

- Benevolence Ministry Team
- Missions Ministry Team
- Music Ministry Team
- Single Adult Ministry Team

The Organizational Manual of the Church discloses all Ministry Teams and their respective Ministry Position Descriptions.

Article VI
Indemnification of Elders, Officers, Employees and Other Agents

Section 1: Definitions
    For the purpose of this Article,

Agent "Agent" means any person who is or was an elder, director, officer, trustee, employee or other agent of the Church, or is or was serving at the request of the Church as an elder, director, officer, trustee, employee or agent of another foreign or domestic corporation, partnership, joint venture, trust or enterprise, or was an elder, director, officer, employee or agent of a foreign or domestic corporation that was a predecessor corporation of the Church or another enterprise at the request of such predecessor corporation.

Proceeding "Proceeding" means any threatened, pending or completed action or proceeding whether civil, criminal, administrative or investigative.

Expenses "Expenses" include, without limitation, all attorneys' fees and any other expenses incurred in defense of any claims or proceedings against an agent by reason of his position or relationship as agent and all attorneys' fees, cost, and other expenses incurred in establishing a right indemnification under this Article.

Section 2: Successful Defense of Agent
To the extent that an agent of the Church has been successful on the merits in the defense if any proceeding referred to in this Article, or in the defense of any claim, issue, or matter therein, the agent shall be identified against expenses actually and reasonably incurred by the Agent in connection with the claim. If an agent either settles any such claim or sustains a judgment rendered against him, then the provisions of Sections 3 through 5 of this Article shall determine whether the agent is entitles to indemnification.

Section 3: Actions Brought by Persons Other than the Church
Subject to the required findings to be made pursuant to Section 5 below, the Church shall indemnify any person who was or is a party, or is threatened to be made a party, to any proceeding other than action brought by, or in the right of, the Church, to procure judgment on its favor, an action brought under State or Federal law, by reason of the fact that such person is or was an agent of the Church for all expenses, judgments, fines, settlements, and other amounts actually an d reasonably incurred in connection with the proceeding.

Section 4: Action Brought by or on Behalf of the Church
Claims Settled Out of Court If any agent settles or otherwise disposes of a threatened or pending action brought by or on behalf of the Church, without court approval, the agent shall receive no indemnification for either amounts paid pursuant to the terms of the settlement or other disposition or for any expenses incurred in defending against the proceeding.

Threatened Pending or Completed Actions Against Agent The Church shall indemnify any person who was or is a party or is threatened to be made a party to any threatened, pending or completed action brought by or in the right of the Church, or brought under the State or Federal law, to procure a judgment in its favor, by reason of the fact that the person is or was an agent of the Church, for all expenses actually reasonably incurred in connection with the defense or settlement of that action, provided that both the following are met:

1. The determination of good faith conduct required by The determination of good faith conduct required by Section 5 below, must be made in the manner provided for in that section; and
2. Where the agent has actually been adjudged liable to the church in performance of such person's duty to the Church, unless, and only to the extent that the court in which such proceedings is or was pending, shall, upon application, determine that, in view of all of the circumstances of the case, the agent is fairly and reasonably entitled to indemnity for the expenses incurred. If the agent is found to be entitled, the court shall determine the appropriate amount of expenses to be reimbursed.

Section 5: Determination of Agent's Good Faith Conduct
The indemnification granted to an agent in Section 3 and 4 of the Article is conditioned on the following:

Required Standard of Conduct The agent seeking reimbursement must be found, in the manner provided below, that he acted in good faith, in a manner he believed to be in the best interest of the Church, and with such care, including reasonable inquiry as an ordinary prudent person in a like position would use in similar circumstances. The termination of any proceeding by judgment, order, settlement, conviction, or on a plea of nolo contendere or its equivalent, shall not, of itself, create a presumption that the person did not act in good faith or in a manner which he reasonably believed to be in the best interest of the Church or that he had responsible cause to believe that his reasonable cause to believe that his conduct was unlawful.

Manner of Determination of Good Faith Conduct The determination that the agent did act in a manner complying with Section 5 above shall be made by:

1. The elders by a majority vote of a quorum consisting of elders who are not parties to the proceeding; or
2. Approval of Church members, with the persons to be indemnified not being entitled to vote thereon; or
3. The court in which the proceeding is or was pending. Such determination may be made on application brought by the Church or the agent or the attorney or the other person rendering a defense to the agent whether or not the application by the agent, attorney or other person is opposed by the Church.

Section 6: Limitations

No indemnification or advance shall be made under this Article, except as provided in <u>Sections 2 or 5</u>, in any circumstances when it appears:

1. That the indemnification or advance would be inconsistent with a provision of this Article of Incorporation, the Bylaws, a resolution of the Board of Elders, Executive Council or Church members, or an agreement in effect at the time of the accrual of the alleged cause of action asserted in the proceeding in which the expenses were incurred or other amounts were paid, which prohibits or otherwise limits indemnification; or
2. That the indemnification would be inconsistent with any condition expressly imposed by a court in approving a settlement.

Section 7: Advance of Expenses

Expenses incurred in defending any proceeding may be advanced by the Church before the final disposition of the proceedings on receipt of an undertaking by or on behalf of the agent to repay the amount of the advance unless it is ultimately determined that the agent is entitles to be indemnified as authorized in this Article.

Section 8: Insurance

The Executive Council may adopt a resolution authorizing the purchase and maintenance of insurance on behalf of any agent of the Church against any liability asserted against or incurred by the agent in such capacity or arising out of the agent's status a s such, whether or not the Church would have the power to indemnify the agent; provided, however, that the Church shall have no power to purchase and maintain such insurance to indemnify any agent of the Church for violation of State or Federal laws.

Article VII
<u>Binding Arbitration</u>

Members of ABC-Church believe that Scripture teaches Matthew 18:15-20 and I Corinthians 6:1-8 that every effort must be made to live at peace and resolve disputes or conflicts with each other in private or within the Church. Therefore, the members of ABC-Church agree that any claim or dispute arising from or related to being a member of ABC-Church, which claim or dispute is not resolved between the parties through the use of principles set forth in Matthew 18, shall be settled by biblically based and legally binding arbitration in accordance with the *Rules of Procedure for Christian Conciliation* of the Institute for Christian Conciliation. Judgment upon an arbitration award may be entered in any court having jurisdiction. Members understand that these methods shall be sole remedy for any controversy or claim arising out of their church membership shall be the sole remedy for any controversy or claim arising out of their Church membership and expressly waive their right to file any suit or claim against one another for such cla9ims or disputes, except to enforce an arbitration decision or provisions of this article.

Article VIII
Ordaining, Licensing and Commissioning

Section 1: Ordaining and Licensing of Ministers

Any present member of this Church, or former member now serving in the ministry at another location, who by his piety, zeal, and aptness to preach and teach gives evidence that he is called of God to the work of the ministry may, by vote of majority of the members present at any regular Church meeting, and after examination by the Senior Minister and elders as his Christian experience, be ordained or licensed by the Church to the Christian Ministry.

When a Church of a like faith and order shall have called a member of this Church to its staff and shall have requested in writing that be ordained, this Church shall consider such request. If the Church by a vote of majority of the members present at a regular Church meeting approves such a request, then it shall authorize and direct Senior Minister to assemble an ordination council of ordained ministers of the Gospel of the like faith and order and elders of like faith and order shall perform the ceremony of ordaining this member to the Gospel Ministry in the name of, and in the presence of the Church.

Section 2: Ordaining Deacons

If the Church, at a regular Church meeting, shall elect a member of members to the scriptural office of deacon, it shall authorize and direct the Senior Minister to assemble an ordination council which may be composed of ordained ministers of the Gospel of like faith and order, elders and deacons of this Church, and visiting elders and deacons of like faith and order who shall perform the ceremony of ordaining him or them to the office of deacon, in the name of, and in the presence of, this Church.

Section 3: Commissioning of Missionaries

Any present member of this Church, or former member now serving in ministry at another location, who by his or her leading and convictions feel called of God to work of missions may, by vote of a majority of the members present at any regular Church meeting, and after examination by the Senior Minister and Missions Ministry Team as to his or her Christian experience, be commissioned by the Church to missionary related services.

Article IX
Fiscal Year

The Fiscal year of the Church shall begin on January 1 and end December 31 of each year.

Article X
<u>Integrated Auxiliary Ministries</u>

Every ministry organization or society within this Church will be an integral part of the Church and not an entity itself. They shall, therefore, have their aims and objectives that of assisting the Church in discharging the obligations and responsibilities, which it has imposed upon itself, rather than having separate aims and objectives, which usually act as divisive forces. The elders will preside over all such integrated auxiliary ministries, and may develop additional ministries as the inclusive because of the rapid growth of the Church:

- The First Bookstore
- Bus Ministry
- Child Enrichment Center
- Crisis Pregnancy Center
- First Academy
- Mom's Day Out

Article XI
<u>Fiscal Responsibilities</u>

Section 1: Accounts, Books and Records
ABC-Church shall maintain adequate and accurate books and records of accounts (financial records; written minutes of the proceedings of its members, Board of Elders, staff, councils and committees; records of the membership of Church, setting forth the members' names and addresses; and contribution records of contributors. All such records shall be kept at its principal place of business. The adequacy and accuracy of these records shall be overseen by the Executive Council.

Section 2: Organizational and Policies and Procedures Manuals
These manuals have been prepared as a guide to all who serve in a leadership position at ABC-Church. Their purpose is to aid in the effective and efficient functioning of individuals and groups and to optimize the fulfilling of ABC-Church's purpose. They provide guidelines and summary information about the Church's organizational structure and ministry operations.

Policy statements will be prepared by those leaders who are responsible for the various Church ministry operations. The procedures will be primarily prepared by staff and committee who are charged with carrying out such ministry operations in accordance with the policies. Policy statements should never become "canonized" and dictate but rather they should guide and protect. The Executive Council, who is primary body who oversees the Church's operations, will guard against policy statements which perpetuate emphases on yesterday and tradition, thwart invocative proposals, and inhabit efforts to build culturally appropriate ministries. Policies and procedures will be designed to provide reasonable assurance that the established ministry objectives/goals/values of ABC-Church will be achieved in an orderly and timely fashion.

If a conflict between doctrine, philosophy of ministry, Church policies, operating procedures, position descriptions, or any other related organizational or operational matters of the Church arise, the content in these manuals should address an appropriate method for solution. If these manuals do not address the conflict, then it should be addressed with the Executive Council.

The Board of Elders reserves the right to modify, supplement, rescind, or revise any of the manuals' information from time to time, with or without notice, as they feel necessary and appropriate as so led by the Lord and Savior Jesus Christ, who is the Head of this body of believers.

These manuals shall be maintained by the staff person charged with administration and shall consist of following sections:

Organizational Manual
Section I   Constitution (Philosophy of Ministry)
Section II   Primary Governing Documents
Section III   Organizational Charts of Leadership and Ministry Structure
Section IV   Leadership Position Descriptions
Section V   Ministry Descriptions

Policies and Procedures Manual
Section I   Leadership and Management
Section II   Personnel
Section III   Financial
Section IV   Facilities
Section V   General Administration
Section VI   Ministry

Section 3: Inspection of Records, Reports and Documentation
Every active/resident member shall have the absolute right, at any reasonable time, to inspect all records, records and documentation of every kind (with the exception of personnel salaries, contribution records and confidential counseling sessions) and the physical properties of ABC-Church. The Executive Council, if necessary to maintain good order, may restrict and limit the number of inspections or establish an orderly manner for such to be conducted. But in no event shall a reasonable inspection of the books and records be denied to a member.

A copy of the Organizational Manual and Policies and Procedures Manual is maintained in the Church Office for inspection by Church members.

Section 4: Internal Auditing/Safety Committee
The Board of Elders will establish and Internal Auditing /Safety Committee for the purpose of providing: assurance that the Church is operating its activates in an effective and efficient manner which demonstrates the wise stewardship of time and material resources; assurance that key risk areas of the Church are being managed by the use of adequate internal controls in its operational systems; assurance that the financial disclosures made by the staff and Finance committee of the Church reasonably portray the ministry's financial condition, results of operations, cash flows needs, and long-term commitments; and assurance that the Church is in reasonable compliance with pertinent laws and regulations, is conducting its affairs ethically, and is maintaining effective controls against leadership and employee conflicts-of-interest.

Throughout the year, this committee will continue to review the organizational structure and operational systems of the Church to accomplish the assurances mentioned above. They will work closely with the staff, Executive Council and Standing Committees of the Church. They will report directly to the Board of Elders regarding their findings.

Article XII
Amendments to the Bylaws

These Bylaws or any provision of them may be altered, amended or repealed, and new Bylaws may be adopted at any time by the Board of Elders, with affirmation of change, as reflected by two-thirds (2/3) vote of the members present at any special or regular membership meeting at which a quorum is present.

IMPORTANT NOTICE TO CHURCH LEADERS

This resource has been prepared solely for illustrative purposes. The resource is not intended to be all-inclusive with regard to laws and regulations under no circumstances should it be relied upon for that purpose. Furthermore, because laws and regulations do frequently change and vary from one state to another, some materials in this resource may be outdated or not applicable. The services of competent accounting, legal, or other professional advisors always be sought to standards, laws, and regulations that directly relate to your church.

NOTES

_____
_____
_____
_____

<h1 style="text-align:center;">501 (c) (3) Non-Profit Religious Organizations
Tax and Legal Issues
for Churches
Attorney Uleses Henderson Jr. Esq</h1>

OVERVIEW
Corporate Structure
Board of Directors
Employee Compensation
Housing Allowances
Other Tax Concerns
Employee Training
Intellectual Property Issues
Insurance

CORPORATE STRUCTURE
Religious Non-Profit Organizations
Churches are religious non-profit organizations
For profit vs non-profit organizations
- Both for profit and non-profit organizations are allowed by law to earn profit at the entity level.
- **For profit organizations exists** to operate a business to generate profit for the benefit of those who own the enterprise (private inurement: ways of transferring an organizations net earrings to persons in private capacity)
- **Non-profit organizations** are required to use their profits for their program activities (i.e., their exempt functions), and may not engage in acts of private inurement
- The assets of corporation of a corporation formed for charitable of public purposes are **irrevocably dedicated** to charitable purposes.
- The corporation **must** use the assets for the states purpose and upon dissolution; **many only** distribute the assets to an organization having similar purposes.

OWNERSHIP/CONTROL
- For the most part, non-profit organizations do not have owners who would be comparable to stockholders (for-profit); they function for the benefit of the public.
- Usually, the control of non-profit organizations is vested in its governing body, frequently termed a **BOARD OF DIRECTORS** or **BOARD OF TRUSTEES.**
Governance and control of organizations usually set forth in the bylaws.

> Document (separate form articles of organization) containing rules in which an organization conducts its affairs.

EXEMPT ORGANIZATIONS

The concept of the **NON-PROFIT ORGANIZATION** is different from that of **TAX-EXEMPT ORGANIZATION**
> The term tax-exempt means an organization that is exempt, in whole or in part, from paying federal income tax

Are all non-profit organizations at-exempt?
> NO!
> You are not automatically tax exempt just because you are structured as a non-profit organization
> The organization must meet specific statutory and other regulatory as non-profit organization

Most tax-exempt organizations under the federal law are those that are described in Section 501 (c) (3) of the Internal Revenue Code
> Most common is the 501 (c) (3) for charitable, religious, and educational organizations

Are churches **REQUIRED** to file tax-exempt status?
> NO! Churches are tax-exempt by law.
> Churches are not required to file for tax-exempt (e.g., 501 (c) (3) tax-exempt recognition
> This also applies to jurisdictions (automatically tax-exempt)

Should I think about obtaining tax-exempt recognition anyway?
> YES, there are certain benefits
> Assures donors that their contributions are deductible as charitable gifts
> Exemption from federal and state income tax
> May be exempt from certain employment taxes
> Determination letter-corp donations
> Enables organizations to be eligible for various non-profit mailing privileges
> Some bans require this to secure collateral to church property

BUT REMEMBER: If you file and are recognized as tax-exempt organizations i.e., 501 (c) (3), you must abide by its regulations.
Tax-exempt can be lost:
> Earnings inure to private individuals (s)/ excess compensation) (can pay reasonable salaries to staff)
> Substantial lobbying- attempts to influence legislation (tricky)

- Electioneering-endorsing or opposing any candidate for public office
- Activities that generate too much unrelated business income (UBI)

STATE INCOME TAX-EXEMPTION

- 501 (c)(3) non-profit organizations are eligible for state-exemption from payment of corporate income tax, as well as other tax exemptions and benefits.
- Religious non-profit organizations receive most, if not, all their income in the form of gifts that are excluded from the organization's income.
- Most states expressly exempt religious organizations form tax and corporate income.

HOW DOES ONE OBTAIN 501 (c) (3) STATUS?

Most organizations must submit a detailed application with certain supporting documents. In that application you must show that you meet:

(1) **organizational test** as a church, charitable organizations; and
(2) **operational test** as a church or charitable organization.

- The application is approximately 25-30 pages

The supporting Documents would consist of providing the IRS with:
- A copy of your organizing documents such as your Articles of Incorporation (which must also provide that if your entity was to dissolve, then all its assets must contributed to another 501 (c) (3) or government), bylaws, and financially statements for the past 3 years (unless new corp.)
- Your entire file with the IRS is subject to Public Inspection
- Certain organizations are consisted 501 (c) (3) without having to submit an application, such as churches and conventions or associations of churches.
- However, they are still held to the standard of being: (1) organized as a church and (2) operating as a church

CORPORATE RECORDS

- All tax-exempt organizations, including churches, are requires to maintain books of account and other records necessary to justify their claim for exemption in the event of an audit
  - Also required to maintain books and records that are necessary to accurately file any federal tax and information returns that may be required.

  Types of corporate records that should be maintained at principle office:
- Articles of Incorporation
- Bylaws (including restated and amendments)
- Minutes of all meeting BoDs (minute books by year)
- Record of all actions taken by BoDs w/o a meeting
- Resolutions adapted by the BoDs
- Appropriate accounting records (general ledgers)

- ➢ Receipts and disbursement journals
- ➢ Payroll records, bank records, and invoices
- ➢ Names and addresses of all members of BoDs

PRACTICE POINTER

It is good practice to have the board, committee, and member minutes reviewed, at least initially, to ensure that they are being prepared sufficiently. Experienced lawyers will know to revise them with the view that each document will someday be exhibit in trail.

ANNUAL BUSINESS MEETING

Religious Organizations should hold annual business meetings
- ➢ To provide state and direction of each church
- ➢ Present overview of last year's financials
- ➢ Provide and approve, of required, annual budgets
- ➢ Elect new Board Members

BOARD OF DIRECTORS/TRUSTEES

Role of Board of Directors
- The activated of a nonprofit corporation and all of its corporate powers are existed by or under the direction of a board of directors.
- BoDs do not run day-to-day operations
- BoDs of religious organizations do not exercise spiritual oversight (this is reserved for pastor)
- COGIC is **hierarchical** church: BoD do not manage, hire, or fire pastors (power to appoint reserved to Jurisdictional Bishop)
- Primary Job is to manage church assets

A nonprofit corporation must have a board of directors
- ➢ **Religious organizations may alter this requirement** as well as the scope of authority of a BOD through its articles or bylaws
  Persons who serve as directors make corporate decisions **collectively** as a board or as committee of board
- ➢ Directors **not required** to fulfill responsibilities or exercise powers **directly**; may delegate to others (e.g., committees) so long as actions remain subject to board direction and control
- ➢ **PRACTICE POWER:** Must keep minutes of all committee and subcommittee meetings

- You must keep records of EVERY meeting of the BoDs because EVERY action of the Board, especially resolutions, must be supported SOURCE DOCUMENTATION (e.g., meeting minutes)

- Without a source document, IRS will not recognize the action
- For example: setting the pastor's salary, there must be meeting minutes that discuss how the salary was determined

This protects the Board from personal liability

- Being a member of BoD is not just a title, it is a responsibility!
- All BoDs have a **fiduciary duty**: this is a legal relationship of trust and confidence between the Board and the members it serve.
- Standard is **prudence:** acting with the same degree of judgment is administering the affairs of organization as they would their personal affairs.
- Written resolution and proper board minutes tend to show that the Board acted in good faith in carrying our its fiduciary duties and responsibilities/ provide the details of actions being taken by the board

All BoDs owe a duty of care to organizations
- Require that all BoDs be reasonable informed about
- Organizations activities
- Participate in making decisions
- Do so good faith and with the care of an ordinary prudent person in similar circumstances.

BOARD OF DIRECTORS RESPONSIBILITES

A. Preserving and, when necessary, reshaping the mission
B. Selection of officers and chief executive
C. Ensuring the organization is well managed
D. Protecting the organization and its assets from external threats
E. Exercising financial stewardship/investments
F. Making sure that the board has the right skills and practices to do its job
G. Making sure that the organization is in compliance with laws and regulations

HOW TO SELECT BOARD OF DIRECTORS

A. Normally set forth in bylaws
B. May want to consider rolling Board with 3 to 5 year terms
C. May establish a Board Selection Screening Committee
D. Board Members should comprise persons with diverse professional backgrounds (both secular and religious)
E. Majority of the membership should vote/elect members
A good time to do this is during annual business meeting

PERSONAL RESPONSIBILITY AS BOARD

Your individual service as duties as a Board member include:

- Attendance—You should all board and committee meeting if at all possible.
- **Be prepared and informed**—In preparation for each meeting, read material sent to you by the committee or board chair and by the staff. Come prepared to ask questions and make comments.
- **Speak your mind and ask hard questions**
- **Stewardship of their organization's assets**—The board is responsible for the stewardship of the assets entrusted to the organization. The board must make certain that funds are used consistent with the intent of those who have given the organizations its funds.

Your individual service and duties as a Board member include:

- **Integrity is paramount**—The most important asset of your organization is its good name. The second most important asset is the confidence of its donors and sponsors in the organization's capacity to manage and spend funds prudently.

BOARD ORIENTATION

- Once a board member has been selected, it is important that he or she be brought up to speed as quickly as possible to be able to make a meaningful contribution.
- The **chairperson of the board** should provide a mechanism for board member orientation and development.
- New board members should receive a briefing from the chairperson to help the new board members understand the organization's activities.

BOARD SOURCEBOOK

Ideally, the organization should make available to all board members a "board orientation book" or "sourcebook." A board book could contain the following information:

- The organization's articles of incorporation;
- The bylaws and any amendments;
- A brief history of the organizations;
- A statement of the organization's mission services;
- Regular financial and operating reports from the past year;
- The organization's strategic plan;
- A copy of the directors' offices' (D&O) liability policy;
- Contact sheet listing all the board members, their addresses and phone numbers;
- A list of key executives of the organization;
- Rules about expense reimbursement and, if applicable, expense forms;
- A calendar of all board meetings with dates, time and locations for the coming year;
- Minutes of meetings held within the past year;
- A summary of conflict-of interest policy disclosures; and

- Results of any governmental audits.
- A contact sheet listing all the board members, their addresses and phone numbers;
- A list of key executives of the organization;
- Rules about expense reimbursement and, if applicable, expense forms;
- A calendar of all board meeting with dates, times and locations for the coming year;
- Minutes of meetings held within the past year;
- A summary of conflict-of-interest policy disclosures; and
- Results of any governmental audits.

BOARD MANANGEMENT

It is important for the board and management of the organization to have a **clear understanding** of the distinctive roles of each.

- In general, **boards** reserve from themselves certain functions such as setting board policy, approving new programs or the deletion of old programs, selection, oversight, and compensation of the chief executive, approval of the operating budget recommended by management, and oversight of the endowment.
- **Management,** in general, is responsible for the selection and supervision of staff, the development, recommendation to the board, and the implementation of the budget, and the establishment of operating procedures.

WHAT DOES A BOARD MEETING LOOK LIKE

A. Reading of agenda
B. Review and Approval of Last Meeting Minutes Financials
C. Old (Unfinished) Business
D. New Business
E. Adjournment

EXTERNAL AUDITS

- An external audit by a qualified public accounting firm is **critical to the integrity of the organization** and a **key element** of the board's responsibility.
- **The external auditor is accountable to the board, NOT management**
- The accounting firm should be selected by a audit committee on behalf of the board of directors.
- The accounting firm should present the audited financial statements to the audit committee and the board of directors.

BOARD LIABILITY

1) A board member as a **fiduciary obligation** to the organization. He or she must act with good faith and loyalty, and in the best interest of the organization

2) Board members are subject to statutory liability and tax penalties (excess compensation)
3) A board has a legal duty to conserve and protect the organization's assets
4) Many not-for-profit organizations carry D & O liability insurance to protect their board members from legal liability.
5) A **conflict-of-interest** can also be the basis of liability action against a board member. If a board member receives an **improper or undisclosed personal financial benefit** as a result of the organization's transactions, he or she may be liable to the organization.
6) A conflict of interest arises when a person in a position of authority over an organization, such as an officer, director, or manager, **can benefit financially** from a decisions he or she could make in such capacity, including indirect benefits as to family members or businesses with which the person is closely associated.
7) Need approval of disinterested Board members
8) BEST PRACTICES: **relatives of pastor or current employees of the church should not** serve as board members; **family members should not** serve on board at same time.

BOARD POLICIES
- Conflict of Interest Policy
- Whistleblower Policy
- Document Retention and Destruction Policy
- Joint Venture Policy
  - Ensure all contracts entered into with the organization be on terms that are at arm's length or more favorable to the organization.
- Gift Acceptance Policy
- Form 990 Board Review Policy
- Compensation Policy

EMPLOYEE COMPENSATION
Why Is This Issue Important?
IRS has heightened its security of churches and other non-profit organizations
- IRS has targeted COGIC pastors

In 2009 IRS released new audit guidelines for ministries
- Definition of minister
- Minister employment
- Status
- Minister employment Status
- Minister income/how income reported
- Housing/ parsonage allowance
- Reporting of business expenses

- Social Security (SECA) tax reporting
  - Church can loose its tax-exempt status if IRS determines that employee (pastor's) compensation is excessive
  - Board of Directors/Trustees who approved excessive compensation may be subject to tax penalty

SPECIAL TAX PROVISIONS FOR MINISTERS
1) Exemption from Mandatory Income Tax Withholding
2) Self-Employed Status for Social Security purposes
3) Eligible for Voluntary Income Tax Withholding
4) Possible Exemption from Social Security Coverage
5) Housing Allowance Exclusion
6) Potential "Double-Deduction" of Mortgage Interest and Real Estate Taxes
   - Itemized expense on Schedule A
   - Housing expenses for Housing Allowance

WHO IS A MINISTER?
IRS/U.S. Tax Court's 5-Factor Test (1987)
- Administers sacraments
- Conducts religious worship
- Has management responsibilities in local church or religious denomination
- Is ordained, commissioned, or licensed
- Is considered to be a religious leader by his or her church or denomination

MINISTERS ARE TAX-EXEMPT
- The tax code exempts from income tax withholding wages paid for "services performed by duly ordained, commissioned, or licensed minister of a church in the exercise of his ministry"
- Ministers are exempt from income tax withholding whether they report their income taxes as employees or as self-employed
- Ministers MUST report and prepay their income taxes and self employment (social security) taxes using estimated tax procedure (Form 1040-ES), unless they elect voluntary withholding

VOLUNTARY WITHHOLDING
- Ministers who report their income taxes as employees can enter into voluntary withholding arrangement with their church
- Minister must file Form W-4 with church
- If minister elects voluntary withholding, church is only obligated to withhold minister's income tax liability
- Minister is still required to report and prepay self-employment tax

TAX TIP
- Ministers working for a church should receive a Form W-4 each year if they are employees
- Ministers working for a church should receive a For 1099-MISC each year if they are self-employed (and receive at least $600 in compensation)

AN EMPLYEE OR SELF-EMPLOYED?
- Whether a pastor is an employee or self-employed is a very important question
- Some pastors consider themselves to be under the control of God rather than a local o church board
- Employee classification provided ministers some advantages

MINISTER'S DUAL TAX STATUS
BASIC RULE:
- ➢ Ministers are considered EMPLYEES for federal and state income tax reporting purposes (must pay income taxes); and
- ➢ SELF-EMPLOYED for Social Security purposes (must pay self-employment tax)

REPORTING AS A EMPLOYEE
- Most ministers should report their income taxes as employees because IRS treats most ministers as employees
- Most ministers are also better off reporting as employees since
  - ➢ Value of fringe benefits will be non-taxable
  - ➢ Risk of IRS audit is substantially lower
  - ➢ Avoids additional taxes a penalties applied if IRS reclassifies pastor as an employee

TEST DETERMINING EMPLOYEE STATUS
- "Common law" employee test
- The IRS "20-factor" test
- The U.S. Tax Court "12-Facor" test
- Tax regulations treatment of corporate officers

IMPORTANT FACTORS TO CONSIDER
- Degree of control exercised by employer over details of work performed
- Which party invest in facilities used to perform work
- Opportunity for individual to participate in entity's profits or losses
- Whether work is part of employer's regular business
- Permanency of the relationship
- Relationship that parties believe they created

Shelly v. Commissioner- T.C. Memo 1994-433 (1994)
- U.S. Tax Court fond that a Pentecostal Holiness minister was self-employees rather than an employee for federal income tax reporting purposes
- Court used IRS 7-Factor test
  - Degree of control over details of pastor's work
  - Employer's right to discharge pastor
  - Permanency of relationship

HOW DO YOU DETERMINE PASTOR'S EMPLOYMENT STATUS?
Consult a tax professional
BEST PRACTICE: Pastor should enter into definitive employment agreement with church

FORMS OF COMPENSATION
What is Compensation?
- IRS defines "compensation" to include anything of value that the employee receives or has the right to use
- Definition includes salary, love gifts, housing allowance, health insurance, disability insurance, pension contributions or benefits, and any allowance for anything except expenses paid under a qualified accountable expense reimbursement plan
  - Only exception are tax-free fringe benefits under Section 132

COMPENSATION COMPONENTS
Compensation—CASH
+ Base Salary
+ Housing Allowance or Parsonage Allowance
+ Social Security (SECA) Allowance
+ Other Income—CASHE
+ Compensation—DEFERRED
+ Compensation—BENEFITS
=TOTAL COMPENSATION

COMPENSATION-Cash
- Base salary
- Non-accountable Expense Reimbursement
- Reimbursement of Nondeductible Moving Expenses
- Special Occasion "Gifts" From Church
- Social Security Supplement
- Personal Use of a Church-Provided Automobile
- Premiums on Group-Term Life Insurance in excess of $50,000
  Unrestricted Minister's Discretionary Fund

OTHER FORMS OF INCOME
- Bonuses
- Love/Anniversary Offerings
  - **CAUTION**: Any offerings paid to pastor from church account must be reported by church as taxable income!
- Retirement Gifts over $25 total
- Pastor's wife travel expenses paid by church
- Below market rate interest loans
- Severance Pay

BASE SALARY
Salary
- For IRS purposes, income includes more than the base salary
- A minister's compensation **MUST BE "REASONABLE"**
- Churches that pay "unreasonable compensation" to a minister <u>jeopardize their tax-exempt status</u>

HOW DO YOU KNOW IF COMPENSATION IS REASONABLE?
IRS gives no guidance on issue
- IRS only explains that an excess benefit occurs when an exempt organization pays a benefit to an insider in excess of the value of his or her services
- Income tax regulations define reasonable compensation as "the amount that would ordinarily be paid for like services by the enterprises (whether taxable or tax-exempt) under like circumstance"

WHAT'S REASONABLE COMPENSATION?
In determining reasonableness under the tax code must consider "all economic benefits provided by a tax-exempt organization in exchange for the performance of services."
- All forms of cash and non-cash compensation, including salaries, fees, bonuses, severance payments, and deferred and non-cash compensation; and
- All other compensatory benefits, whether or not included in gross income for income tax purposes, including payments in gross income for income tax purposes, including payments to plans providing medical, dental, or life insurance; disability insurance; taxable and non-taxable fridge benefits

PRESUMPTION OF REASONABLENESS
Compensation is presumed to be reasonable if:
- Compensation arrangement was approved in advance by an authorized body of the tax exemption organization (i.e., board of directors or trustees)

- Authorized body obtained and relied upon appropriate "comparability data" prior to making the determination; and
- Authorized body adequately documented basis for its determination at the time it was made
- If church meets these requirements, burden shifts to IRS to prove compensation was unreasonable

TAX ON MANAGERS

- "Managers" who approve an excess benefit transaction are subject to excise tax equal to 20% of amount of excess benefit—up to maximum of %20K
- Manger" includes any office, director, or trustee of organization, or anyone having similar powers or responsibilities
- Must participate in decision to pay excessive compensation
- Manager can avoid taxation if it relied on advice of legal counsel

WHAT ABOUT PAYING PASTOR PERCENTAGE OF REVENUE?

People of God Community v. Commissioner, 75 T.C, 127 (1980)
- Tax Court revoked exempt status on grounds that it paid 3 ministers a percentage of gross revenue
  - Salaries totaled 86% of organizational budget
  - Amount of each salary was well in excess of average salary of comparable ministers

Compensation based on percentage of income MAY be reasonable and appropriate so long as the amount of compensation paid to minister is reasonable (be careful of private inurement)

IRS Standard: must consider "all relevant facts and circumstances"
- Relationship between size of the benefit provided and quality and quantity of services provided
- Ability of person receiving compensation to control the activities generating the revenues on which compensation is based

HYPO #1

Pastor C serves a church with a congregation of 300 members. His annual compensations is one-half of all church income. This year the church's income was $600,000 and Pastor C was paid $300,000

Reasonable?
- Probably not
- Salary not based or proportional to quantity or quality of services provide
- NOTE: Board could be subject to tax penalty

THE PASTOR'S COMPETENCY MANUAL

HYPO #2
Pastor C servers a church with a congregation of 200 members and annual revenue of $300,000. Under his compensation arrangement, Pastor receives annual salary of $50,000 and a bonus of $15,000 if membership or revenue increases by 10% in a any year.
Reasonable?
- Probably
- Bonus based on performance

PRACTICAL TIPS I. DETERMINING SALARY
Assemble committee of disinterested members of the board of directors (i.e. persons having no conflict of interest) to negotiated and approve pastor's compensation
- Pastor, nor any of his family members or church employees should be part of committee
- Recommendation should be based on formal compensation survey prepared by an accounting firm or tax specialist
- In revenue under $1M, church may survey minister compensation from 3 or more comparable churches
- Document the board's adoption of the pastor's compensation in the meeting minutes and keep copy of compensation survey on file

HYPOTHETICAL SALARY GUIDELINES

Church revenue	Pastor's Salary
$500K and Below	20% to 25%
$500K to $1M	15% to 20%
$1M to $5M	10% to 15%
$5M to 10M	7% to 10%
$10M or More	4% to 7%

**These numbers are purely hypothetical. You must consult a tax professional before determining a PASTOR'S base salary.

HOUESING/CAR/SOCIAL SECRITY ALLOWANCES
Housing Allowance
- *Clergy are entitled to special tax loophole—amounts spent on housing are excluded from their taxable income; they receive the funds but are not required to declare the funds are taxable income*
- *This is the **most significant** tax benefit enjoyed by ministers, yet many ministers fail to claim them or do not claim enough*

- *Applies to ministers who either rent or own homes Parsonage or equity allowances apply to ministers living in church-owned property*
- *Housing Allowance is **ONLY** exclusion for income tax reporting, ministers CANNOT exclude a housing allowance when computing self-employment (Social Security) taxes unless they are retired*
- *MINISTER decides this amount, not the congregation!*
- *Your board of directors or congregation **MUST** annually approve the amount pastor designates and it must be recorded in the official minutes*

HOUSING ALLOWANCE ECLUSION

Housing Allowance may not accept the lowest of the following amounts:
- *Amount designated by church*
- *Actual housing expenses*
- *Fair rental value (FRV) of home (furnished and including utilities). Allowance cannot be adjusted during the taxable year—must be fixed in advance*

BEWARE: if allowance exceeds pastor's actual housing expenses, pastors MUST claim the excess as taxable income

QUALIFYING HOUSING EXPENSES

- *Down payment on a home*
- *Mortgage loan payments (to purchase or improve home)*
- *Rent payments*
- *Real estate taxes*
- *Property insurance*
- *Utilities (electricity, gas, water, trash pickup, and local telephone charges; Internet access fees)*
- *Furnishings and appliances (purchase and/or repair)*
- *Structural repairs and remodeling*
- *Yard maintenance and improvements*
- *Maintenance items (household cleaners, light bulbs, pest control, etc.)*
- *Homeowners association duties*
- *Cable television fee*

HOUSING ALLOWANCE REQUIREMENTS

- *Designation must be in writing*
- *Adopted by the church board or congregation and recorded in minutes*
- *Must be done yearly, in advance of the calendar year—amount should be revised annually*
- ***TIP:** Put housing allowance review on the agenda for every December board/trustee meeting!*

HYPO #3
A pastor earns an annual salary of $42,000 and designates $12,000 as housing allowance in January, When the pastor totals all receipts on housing at the end of the year, the actual amount spent on housing was $10,500.

How much can the pastor exclude from taxable income as non-taxable housing allowance?
Answer: *$10,500, the smaller of the designated amount of the actual.*

CARE ALLOWANCES
Three General Types
- Church provided (leases) car for pastor for his personal and business use throughout year
- Church provided pastor a lump sum to cove automobile expenses
- Church reimburses pastor for expenses
- BE CAREFUL: Minster's personal use of church-provided car must be valued and reported to IRS by BOTH church and minister as taxable income

HYPO #4
Pastor H is given a monthly car allowance of $300 by his church but he is not required to substantiate the business purpose of amount of any of his business expenses.

Is this proper?
Classic example of non-accountable reimbursement arrangement (taxable income)
- Church must report all monthly allowances (3,600) on Pastor's W-2
- Pastor must report all monthly allowances as income on Form 1040; and
- Pastor may deduct actual expenses ONLY as miscellaneous itemized deduction on Schedule A

SOCIAL SECURITY ALLOWANCE
- *Employees of a business MUST pay FICA tax (under Federal Insurance Contribution Act). Normally employer pays 50% and employees pays 50%. In 2009 the rate was 15.3%*
- *Pastors are <u>self-employed for Social Security purposes</u> and are required to pay 15.3% SECA tax (Self-Employment Contributions Act) on full salary (including amounts designated as housing allowance)*
- *A church may choose to pay 50% of pastor's SECA=7.65% ("employer's" portion): some may pay the full amount.*
- *Whatever is paid by church is included in pastor's total compensation*

DEFERRED COMPENSATION
- *Annuities*
  - 403 (b) tax-sheltered
- *Pensions*

- *Individual Retirement Arrangement (IRAs)*
- *Rabbi Trust*
- *401 (k) plans*
- *Keogh plans (for self-employed ministers)*
  - *Pension for organizations that consist of 10 or fewer employees who are highly paid ($100,000)*

RABBI TRUST
- *An irrevocable trust where a portion of pastor's salary is deferred and held in trust*
- *Funds transferred to trust not taxable to rabbi (pastor)*
- *Trust cannot be assigned to used by pastor as collateral*
- *Trust MUST provide that trust assets are subject to general creditors of employer*
- *Useful because with proper drafting it allows church to set aside amounts in trust that exceed limits associated with other retirement plans*
- *Before establishing rabbi trust consult attorney to ensure compliance worth tax regulations*

BENEFITS PACKAGES
Compensation – Benefits
- *Annuity- 403 (b) tax-sheltered*
- *Health Insurance (Dental, Vision, Health)*
- *Disability Income and Term Life Insurance Plan (premiums must not excess $50,00)*
- *Group Life Insurance*
- *Annual Health Examination*
- *Medicare (when pastor reaches the age 65)*
- *Worker's Compensation*
- *Malpractice Insurance*
- *Key Man Insurance (allotment to pastor's heirs)*
- *Vacation*
- *Sick Days*
- *Parental Leave (birth/adoption)*
- *Sabbatical Leave (spiritual/intellectual enrichment)*
- *Personal Days*
- *Continuing Education) (study leave)*
- *Death Leave*
- *Child Care Allowance*

RETIREMENT PACKAGES
- *403 tax-sheltered annuities*
- *Qualified pension plan*
- *Simple Employee Pension Plan (SEP)*

- *IRAs (Roth / Traditional)*
- *Church retirement income accounts*
- *Rabbi trust*
- *Other options*
- *Retirement stipend (% of salary)*
- *Health Insurance (pastor/spouse)*
- *Stipend for surviving spouse*

SERMON/MEDIA SALES AND OWNERSHIP
Media Sales
- *It is reasonable to provide a royalty (commission) to pastor for sermon sales*
  - *% of gross*
  - *% of net sales*
- *Media sales is taxable for pastor*
- *NOTE: Book sales (ebooks) often controlled by pastor and/or pastor's publisher*

COPYRIGHT INTEREST IN A SERMON
- *Two forms of copyright interest in a sermon*
  - *Underlying work (e.g., sermon notes, outline)*
  - *Master recording (i.e., performance of the work)*
    - *Tape, CD, DVD*

WHO OWNS COPYRIGHTS IN SERMONS?
- **Conservative (Traditional) View**
  - *Pastor owns all rights*
  - *Inspired by God*
- **Liberal (Corporate) View**
  - *Church owns all rights*
  - *Pastor is employee*
- **Legal Default (Hybrid View)**
  - *Pastor owns rights to underlying work*
  - *Church owns rights to masters*
- **POSSIBLE SOLUTION**
- *Pastor owns all rights to sermons (both underlying work and masters)*
- *Pastor gives church an exclusive license to sell master recordings of sermons for term of pastor's relationship with church*
- *At the end of relationship, license to sell master recordings terminates and all rights revert back to pastor and his heirs*

- Structure agreeable to most BODs
- **PUT IN WRITING**
- Issue of sermon ownership is often unaddressed
- Define ownership rights in an applicable license or assignment
- Can add applicable license or assignment as an exhibit to your employment agreement
- **NOTE:** copyright ownership can ONLY be transferred in writing
- **REIMBURSEMENTS**
- Professional
- Automobile
- Business
- Moving (if applicable)
- Continued Education (study aids, seminars, Bible college)
- Travel
- Ecclesiastical Meetings
- Other Expenses
  - Cleaning vestments
  - Professional Journals
  - Professional dues/jurisdictional and National assessments
- **TRAVEL EXPENSES**
- Hotel (Marriot, Hyatt or equivalent)
- Airfare (first class, business class)
- Frequent flyer points
- Rental Care (town care, SUV, full size)
- Accounting
  - Reimbursement of actual business mileage (commuting mileage is not included) OR
  - Estimated auto allowance agreed on in advance; compare with actual mileage and settle account at tend of year receipts for other travel expenses (parking, tolls)
- **REIMBURSED EXPENSES**
- **CAUTION:** church MUST have an accountable reimbursement policy!
- **OTHER TAX ISSUES**

Anniversary/Love Gifts
- Love gifts are taxable income
- If you want to bless pastor, then you should just put money in his hand (can't hit general church ledger), but you can't claim it as a tax write-off
- **ISSUE:** you can't claim gift as a tax wrote-off unless the pastor claims it as taxable income. If pastor doesn't claim gift as taxable income, it can't be written off. You can't have it both ways.
- **UNRELATED BUSINESS INCOME (UBIT)**

- **What is UBIT?**
  - *Organization may not receive income from a regally carried on trade or business that is not related to its mission.*
  - *If you generate funds from a business activity but it is not regular, you will probably have to pay taxes on that income but it won't jeopardize your tax-exempt status. An example, you could be selling merchandise once a year at a fair.*
  - *If your organization earns more than $100 during the year, it must file IRS from 990-T, Exempt Organization Business Income Tax Return.*
- *Too much UBIT can threaten your tax-exempt status*
  - *Generally, up to 15%-20% without jeopardizing exempt 501 (c)(3) status*
  - *If revenues exceeds this threshold, may be better to establish separate for-profit entity*
- *Example: Bookstore*
  - *Pay sales tax*
  - *Keep separate books from general church ledger*
- *For seasonal products, measuring period (regularity) is duration od season, not year (e.g. selling Christmas trees)*
- **GRANTS**
- *May be booked in general ledger (Fund) as Restricted Funds*
- *You must adhere to grant restrictions and stated purpose to the letter or else you will require to return the money*
- *Officers may also have personal liability and could face jail time if federal grant money is missed is misused/managed*
- **CHARITABLE FUNDRAISING**
- *Are all tax-exempt organizations edible to receive tax-deductible contributions?*
  - *NO. But churches ARE.*
- *UBIT applies in fundraising setting*
  - *But sales from bookstore and gifts shops are considered related businesses*
  - *Other sales in these shops and stores may be nontaxable by operation of convenience doctrine*
- *An unrestricted charitable gift is a gift to be applied towards a charitable purpose, regardless of the business form for the recipient (can be generally used)*
- *A donor restricted gift invokes restrictions for a particular purpose*
  - *Examples: building funds, scholarships, mission*
  - *Must be booked as restricted funds and used for restricted purposes of church may incur some liability for misuse*
- **EMPLOYEE TRAINING**
- *Employee Sensitivity Training*
  - *Sexual Harassment Education*

- *Employee/Volunteer Profiles*
  - *Criminal Background screening*
  - *May be required when working with kids*
  - *Check local state regulations regards the types of screening can legally conduct*
- *Counseling*
  - *Hire or refer parishioners to licensed counselors*
- **INTELLECTUAL PROPERTY –Possible IP Issues**
- *Copyrights*
  - *Use of copy written music on CDs/DVDs*
  - *Christian Copyright Licensing International (CCLI)-can license right to publish overhead print music lyrics, stream or podcast copy-written music, including on DVDs/CDs, copy and share recordings for rehearsal purposes*
  - *Podcasting/Streaming/YouTube*
- *Trademarks*
  - *Church Logo/Acronyms*
  - *Another means to protect goodwill of church*
- *Websites*
  - *Content/website ownership*
  - *Notice and Takedown Agent (ISP)*
- *Blogs/Social Media (Twitter/Facebook)*
  - *Monitoring content/moderator*
- *E-Commence/Online giving*
  - *Privacy/security (privacy policy)*
  - *Payment Card Industry (PCI) Data Security compliance*
  - *Use of costumer list*
- *Work-for-Hire*
  - *Specially commissioned work*
  - *Assignment of ownership rights need to be in writing*
- **INSURANCE-Types of Insurance**
  - *General Liability/Umbrella Liability*
  - *Directors & Officers/Errors & Omissions*
  - *Minister's Professional and Personal Liability*
  - *Employee and Volunteer Dishonesty Liability*
  - *Worker's Compensation*
  - *Sexual Misconduct*
  - *Property Insurance*
  - *Automobile Liability Insurance*
  - *Key Man Insurance*

- Earthquake/Flood/Hurricane
- Special Sports
  - E.g., youth sports leagues
- **HELPFUL RESOURCES**
- *Richard R. Hammar, 2009 Church & Clergy Tax Guide*
- *Richard R. Hammar, The 2009 Compensation Handbook for Church Staff*
- *IRS, Tax Guide for Churches and Religious Organizations (Pub. 828)*
- *IRS, Employer's Tax Guide (Pub. 15, 15-A)*
- *IRS, Social Security and Other Information for Members of the Clergy and Religious Workers (IRS Pub. 517)*

NOTES

Made in the USA
San Bernardino, CA
23 July 2015